The Spokesman
Even unto Gaza
Edited by Tony Simpson
Published by Spokesman for the
Bertrand Russell Peace Foundation
Ken Coates: Editor 1970 to 2010

Spokesman 126   **2014**

CONTENTS

Editorial	3	*Tony Simpson*
Preventing the crime of indifference	5	*Richard Falk*
The killing of Salem Khalil Shammaly	10	*Eran Efrati*
What happened in Khuza'a	13	*Mohammed Omer*
The world on notice	16	*Ahdaf Soueif*
Gaza under attack Summary of findings	19	*Russell Tribunal on Palestine*
Who started the First World War?	34	*John Gittings*
A Pacifist at War	45	*Bertrand Russell*
Africa Genocide	55	*John Daniels*
NATO – NO, TA!	67	*Tony Simpson*
NATO's modest steps	70	*Saskia J Stuiveling Ellen M A van Schoten*
Ice Cream	73	*David Vine*
Insulting Machines	100	*Mike Cooley*
Chrome Dome	102	*Ray Perkins, Jr*
Reviews	112	*Dave Putson Michael Barratt Brown Nicole Morris*

Illustrations: With grateful thanks to Frank Barat, Steve Bell, Martin Rowson and Virginie N'Guyen.

A CIP catalogue record for this book is available from the British Library

Published by the
Bertrand Russell Peace Foundation Ltd.,
Russell House
Bulwell Lane
Nottingham NG6 0BT
England
Tel. 0115 9784504
email:
elfeuro@compuserve.com
www.spokesmanbooks.com
www.russfound.org

Editorial Board:
Michael Barratt Brown
John Daniels
Ken Fleet
Stuart Holland
Henry McCubbin
Abi Rhodes
Regan Scott

FSC Mixed Sources
Product group from well-managed forests and other controlled sources
Cert no. SGS-COC-006541
www.fsc.org
© 1996 Forest Stewardship Council

ISSN 1367 7748   Printed by the Russell Press Ltd., Nottingham, UK   ISBN 978 0 85124 843 1

Horror, then degradation, confront Gaza residents

Editorial
Even unto Gaza

The Russell Tribunal on Palestine met in extraordinary session in Brussels on 25 September 2014, a month after an extended ceasefire was called following Israel's latest, bloodiest, and most protracted onslaught on the people of the Gaza Strip. During 51 days, more than 2,200 people were killed, of whom the overwhelming majority were civilians, including hundreds of children. Tens of thousands of homes were reduced to rubble, while hospitals, schools, infrastructure, businesses and farms were all targeted by the Israeli military.

The jury heard compelling eyewitness and expert testimony. We feature the written submissions of an Israeli and a Palestinian, Eran Efrati and Mohammed Omer, who also gave testimony in person and answered questions from members of the jury. Mr Efrati, a former soldier, recounted the destruction of Shuja'iyya, in the East of Gaza City, the scale of which shocked seasoned military analysts, while Mr Omer, a journalist, focused on Khuza'a in the southern Gaza Strip, which suffered massive damage under Israeli fire.

Two other eyewitnesses, Ashraf Mashharawi and Raji Sourani, despite sustained attempts to do so, were prevented from travelling from Gaza to Brussels to testify in person to the Tribunal. Such prohibitions on Palestinian witnesses have been a recurrent feature of sessions of the Russell Tribunal on Palestine.

Juror Ahdaf Soueif puts the world on notice, notwithstanding the mass killings that have already taken place there, that in Gaza 'we are heading towards crimes of great magnitude'. This latest aggression is one of a series during the last few years, since the siege of Gaza was imposed. As she says, there is time to stop killings and destruction of even greater magnitude being perpetrated in the future. But the world is on notice that it has to act to prevent this happening. Eran Efrati informed the Tribunal that, whilst it was sitting, the Israeli government had agreed a substantial increase in its military budget of some 14 billion shekels (£2.3 billion). They are preparing for the next time.

The Tribunal's preliminary findings propose a range of actions at different levels, including that all European Union member states recognise the state of Palestine. The new government in Sweden has moved swiftly to do so. Now, the UK Parliament has also voted by a large majority to recognise the state of Palestine. When will the British Government do so?

◀ *Mohammed Omer testifies to the Tribunal.*

Certainly, Israel is losing influential support. Sir Richard Ottaway, Chairman of Parliament's Foreign Affairs Committee and formerly MP for Nottingham North, is and remains a lifelong friend of Israel. However, he told the House of Commons that the recent annexation of 950 acres of the West Bank 'outraged him more than anything else in my political life, mainly because it makes me look a fool, and that is something that I resent'. He concluded:

> 'I have to say to the Government of Israel that if they are losing people like me, they will be losing a lot of people.'

Such actions, by themselves, will not prevent the sequel to 'Operation Mighty Cliff', as it was called in Hebrew. (The moniker 'Protective Edge' was spin.) But they are indicative of a change of mood more generally about Israel's recurrent brutal, deadly and illegal behaviour. Calls to account are increasing, including from UN Secretary General Ban Ki-moon. As Richard Falk writes in this issue of *The Spokesman*, the Tribunal's assessment of Israel's behaviour towards the people of Gaza 'will support the long struggle to make the rule of law applicable to the strong as well as the weak'.

> *And Joshua smote them from Kadeshbarnea even unto Gaza,*
> *and all the country of Goshen, even unto Gibeon.*
> *Book of Joshua, chapter 10, verse 41, King James Version*

* * *

Russell's book *Freedom and Organisation* was a discursive attempt to 'trace the main causes of political change during the hundred years from 1814 to 1914'. Published in 1934, it warned that the 'same causes that produced war in 1914 are still operative,' adding that 'unless checked by international control of investment and of raw material, they will inevitably produce the same effect, but on a larger scale.' Such critical reflection has largely been absent from much public commentary on the First World War centenary. However, John Gittings has immersed himself in the historians' discourse, which, as he told the Peace History Conference, 'Alternative Voices of World War One', at London's Imperial War Museum, is rather more informative than what political leaders have dared to say. One prominent alternative voice was that of Russell himself, who speaks to us from the heady days of 1917, when Russia was between revolutions.

Preventing the crime of indifference

Richard Falk

Richard Falk is an international law and international relations scholar who taught at Princeton University for forty years. Since 2002 he has lived in Santa Barbara, California, and taught at the local campus of the University of California in Global and International Studies, and since 2005 chaired the Board of the Nuclear Age Peace Foundation. He was a juror at the Extraordinary Session on Gaza of the Russell Tribunal on Palestine.

On 24 September 2014, a special session of the Russell Tribunal critically scrutinised Israel's summer assault on Gaza, Operation Protective Edge, from the perspective of international law, including the core allegation of genocide. The process involved a series of testimonies by legal and weapons experts, health workers, journalists and others, some of whom directly experienced the fifty days of military assault.

A jury composed of prominent individuals from around the world, known for their moral engagement with issues of the day, assessed the evidence with the help of an expert legal team of volunteers who helped with the preparation of the findings and analysis for consideration by the jury, which deliberated and debated all the issues raised – above all, the question of how to respond to the charge of genocide.

The Russell Tribunal on Palestine was inspired by the original Russell Tribunal, which was held in 1967 at the height of the Vietnam War. Convened by the great English philosopher Bertrand Russell and presided over by Jean-Paul Sartre, those original sessions assessed charges of war crimes committed by the United States in Vietnam. Subsequent tribunals included the Russell Tribunal on Latin America, which investigated the military dictatorships in Argentina, Brazil and Chile. The first Russell Tribunal proceedings on Palestine, convened in the wake of Israel's 2008-09 assault on Gaza, were held in four sessions, from 2010 to 2012.

It should be acknowledged that this latest undertaking was never intended to be a neutral inquiry without any predispositions. The tribunal was held because of the enormity of the devastation and the spectacle of horror associated with high-technology weaponry attacking the civilian population of Gaza, which was locked into a combat zone that left no place to hide. The tribunal was also a response to the failures of the international community to do more to stop the carnage, or even to condemn Israel's disproportionate uses of force against an essentially helpless civilian population that included the targeting of a variety of legally forbidden targets, among them UN buildings used as shelters, residential neighbourhoods, hospitals and clinics, and mosques.

Although the tribunal proceeded from the assumption that Israel was responsible for severe wrongdoing, it made every effort to be scrupulous in the presentation of evidence and the interpretation of applicable international law, and relied on testimony from people with established reputations for integrity and conscience. Among the highlights of the testimony were a report on damage to hospitals and clinics given by Dr. Mads Gilbert, a Norwegian doctor serving in a Gaza hospital during the attacks; Mohammed Omer, a widely respected Gazan journalist who daily reported from the combat zone; Max Blumenthal, a prize-winning journalist who was in Gaza throughout Protective Edge and analysed for the jury the overall political design that appeared to explain the civilian targeting patterns; and David Sheen, who reported in agonising detail on the racist hatred expressed by prominent Israelis during the assault, which was widely echoed by Israelis in the social media and never repudiated by the leadership in Jerusalem.

The jury had little difficulty concluding that the pattern of attack, as well as the targeting, amounted to a series of war crimes that were aggravated by the commission of crimes against humanity. These included the imposition of collective punishment upon the entire civilian population of Gaza, in flagrant and sustained violation of Article 33 of the Fourth Geneva Convention. A further notable legal finding was the rejection of the central Israeli claim that it was acting in self-defence against rocket attacks from Gaza. There are several reasons for reaching this conclusion: under international law, the claim of self-defence cannot be used in justifying response to resistance mounted by an occupied people, and from the perspective of international law, Gaza remains occupied due to persisting Israeli control despite Israel's purported 'disengagement' in 2005 (more properly characterised as a military redeployment). The rockets fired from Gaza were at least partly a response to prior Israeli unlawful provocations, including the mass detention of several hundred people loosely associated with Hamas in the West Bank, and the incitement to violence against Palestinians as revenge for the murder of three kidnapped Israeli settler children. And finally, the minimal damage done by the rockets – seven civilian deaths over the entire period – is too small a security threat to qualify as an 'armed attack,' as is required by the UN Charter to uphold a claim of self-defence. At the same time, the jury did not doubt that rocket fire by Palestinian militants into Israel was unlawful, as the rockets were incapable of distinguishing between military and civilian targets.

Much of the concern in the jury deliberations before and after the proceedings themselves was how to address the allegation of genocide, which has been described as 'the crime of crimes'. The jury was sensitive to the differences between the popular and political uses of the word 'genocide,' to describe various forms of collective violence directed at ethnic and religious minorities, and the more demanding legal definition of genocide, which requires compelling evidence of specific 'intent to destroy'.

The testimony made this issue complex and sensitive. It produced a consensus on the jury that the evidence was sufficient to make it appropriate to give careful consideration as to whether the crime of genocide had actually been committed by Israel. This was itself an acknowledgment that there was a genocidal atmosphere in Israel, in which high-level officials made statements supporting the destruction or elimination of the Gazans as a people. Such inflammatory assertions were at no time repudiated by the leadership of Prime Minister Benjamin Netanyahu or subject to criminal investigation, let alone any other official proceedings. Furthermore, the sustained bombardment of Gaza, under circumstances where the population had no opportunity to leave or to seek sanctuary within the Gaza Strip, lent further credibility to the charge. The fact that Operation Protective Edge was the third large-scale, sustained military assault on this unlawfully blockaded, impoverished and endangered population also formed part of the larger genocidal context.

Despite these factors, there were legal doubts as to the crime itself. The political and military leaders of Israel never explicitly endorsed the pursuit of genocidal goals, and they purported to seek a ceasefire during the military campaign. The tribunal convincingly documented the government's goal of intensifying the regime of collective punishment, but there was no clear official expression of intent to commit genocide. The presence of genocidal behaviour and language, even if used in government circles, is not by itself sufficient to conclude that Protective Edge, despite its enormity, amounted to the commission of the crime of genocide.

What the jury did agree upon, however, was that some Israeli citizens and leaders appear to have been guilty in several instances of the separate crime of *incitement* to genocide, which is specified in Article 3(c) of the Genocide Convention. It also agreed that the additional duty of Israel and other parties to prevent genocide, especially the United States and Europe, was definitely engaged by Israeli behaviour. In this regard, the Russell Tribunal is sending an incriminating message of warning to Israel and an appeal to the UN and the international community to uphold the Genocide Convention, and to prevent any further behaviour by Israel that would cross the line.

Many will react to this assessment of Protective Edge as without legal authority and dismiss it as merely recording the predictable views of a 'kangaroo court'. Those allegations have been directed at the Russell Tribunal ever since its founding nearly fifty years ago. Bertrand Russell called the original proceedings a stand of citizens of conscience 'against the crime of silence'. This latest session of the tribunal has a similar mission in relation to Israel's actions in Gaza, although less against silence than indifference. Such tribunals, created almost always in exceptional circumstances and in response to defiance of the most elemental constraints of international law, make crucial contributions to public awareness – especially when geopolitical realities preclude established institutional procedures, such as recourse to the International Criminal Court and the UN Security Council and General Assembly.

When the interests of the West are at stake, as in Ukraine, there is no need to activate unofficial international law initiatives. However, in the case of Israel-Palestine, when the US government and most of Western Europe stand fully behind whatever Israel chooses to do, the need for an accounting is particularly urgent, even if the prospects for accountability are minimal. The long-suffering people of Gaza have endured three criminal assaults in the past six years, which have left virtually the entire population, especially young children, traumatised by the experience.

The Russell Tribunal is filling a normative vacuum in the world. It does not pretend to be a court. In fact, among its recommendations is a call on the Palestinian Authority to join the International Criminal Court and present its grievance to the authorities in The Hague for their investigation and possible indictments. Even then, prosecution will be impossible, as Israel is not a party to the treaty establishing the ICC and would certainly refuse to honour any arrest warrants issued in The Hague. A trial could not proceed without the physical presence of those accused. It is notable that Hamas has joined in urging recourse to the ICC despite the distinct possibility that allegations against its rocket fire would also be investigated and its officials could be indicted for alleged war crimes.

As with the Nuremberg judgment, which documented Nazi criminality but excluded any consideration of the crimes committed by the victors in World War Two, the Russell Tribunal process was flawed and can be criticised as one-sided. At the same time, I am confident that, on balance, this assessment of Israel's behaviour toward the people of Gaza will support the long struggle to make the rule of law applicable to the strong as well as the weak.

With grateful acknowledgements to The Nation, *where this article first appeared.*
www.thenation.com
http://richardfalk.wordpress.com/

COMMUNICATION WORKERS UNION

End the siege on Gaza

Recognise the state of Palestine

Billy Hayes
General Secretary

Beryl Shepherd
President

The Killing of Salem Khalil Shammaly

Testimony of Eran Efrati

Eran Efrati was a sergeant in the Israeli Defense Force, and has been researching the Israeli military since 2008. He brought to light soldiers' testimonies about the use of white phosphorous in Operation 'Cast Lead' in 2008/9, and his investigative reports on the operation were published in the Goldstone report for the UN. During Operation 'Defensive Edge', he collected testimonies along the Gaza border.

Shuja'iyya is a neighbourhood in the East of Gaza City, home to almost 100,000 residents. It is one of the most impoverished and densely populated neighbourhoods in Gaza. Between July 19th and 23rd, 2014, the height of the massacre in Shuja'iyya, it is estimated that between 90 and 120 Palestinians were killed and 400 more were injured. The dead included at least 22 children, 19 women and seven elderly Palestinians. 884 buildings were hit by the Israeli Defense Force (IDF); 604 were utterly destroyed. During operation 'Defensive Edge', the facilities of the United Nations Relief and Works Agency (UNRWA) were overflowing, so the Shuja'iyya residents fleeing the bombing could not find shelter.

The Golani Brigade of the IDF was the first to enter the neighbourhood on the night of 19 July 2014, and was met with resistance. It thus requested backup, which arrived in the form of 600 tank shells as well as aerial bombing. An M-113 armoured vehicle of the IDF was targeted and hit, causing the death of seven combatants from the Golani Brigade. Later on that day, six more Golani soldiers were killed in the fighting, a rare occurrence during recent offensives in Gaza. During the combat, according to IDF officials, IDF forces dropped one ton bombs on at least 120 separate targets from the air. The armoured corps, advancing into the neighbourhood on 20 July, received the order to 'open fire at anything that moved'. At the same time, a military spokesperson announced that Israel would be 'taking off the gloves' in Shuja'iyya. A senior military official told the press that the IDF would be pursing the 'Dahiya Doctrine', referring to a method used by the IDF in Beirut in 2006, whereby the neighbourhood of Dahiya was bombed intensively following the capture of two Israeli soldiers.

According to Pentagon reporting, as relayed by an American military officer, eleven battalions deployed 258 artillery pieces and fired 7,000 shells into the neighbourhood, 4,800 of which were shot in the course of seven hours. Another American expert claimed the only explanation for such use of firepower was 'to kill a lot of people in as short a time as possible'.

On 20 July, soldiers from the Golani Brigade, along with two other units and covered by the armoured corps and the air force, advanced into the neighborhood and captured houses as bases. I collected testimonies independently from three soldiers who were stationed in two of these houses. Two of them are Golani combatants, stationed in the house from which Salem Shammaly would later be shot, and would witness the killing first hand. The third is an officer stationed with his soldiers in a house two buildings to the east, and would also witness the killing first hand.

Upon capturing the houses, the first order was to break the floor tiles so as to use the sand underneath them for sand bags to shield the windows. The second was to clear the main living room of all Palestinian belongings and to throw them into a back room. The third was to create guarding stations; two at the main entrance to the house, one at the back, and three at the front windows. The fourth was to create a 'sniper's position' by breaking a narrow hole in the exterior wall under one of the windows, and to position a sniper there. Finally, the commanding officers drew an invisible red line on the ground between two houses amidst the rubble, which all soldiers would identify as the 'death line' – a line that whoever crosses it is deemed a danger to the soldiers and is therefore to be killed immediately by shooting to the centre of his body. Three of the soldiers who spoke to me relayed that already then it seemed strange to them that the 'death line' was drawn quite far, several hundred metres, from the house in which they were stationed. While a 'death line' has been previously used by the IDF, it has seldom been drawn so far from the soldiers.

The soldiers were then asked to wait for further orders. At 10am they received a briefing, in which they were officially told something that had until then been said only informally. They were told that the officers understood their frustration and their pain at the loss of their fellow soldiers, that they did not die in vain, and that they would soon have a chance to 'take out' this frustration and to avenge the death of their friends.

At 12 midday a new order was given, declaring that a ceasefire would take effect at 1pm. The soldiers began preparations for the ceasefire.

According to Hesham Naser Shammaly, his family stayed behind to protect their valuable clothing stock. As a consequence, his uncle, aunt and two cousins were shot by the IDF. His father was also shot as he tried to speak to approaching soldiers, but survived. During the ceasefire later that afternoon, his cousin, Salem Shammaly, 23, returned home to the neighbourhood to look for surviving relatives amidst the rubble. As he approached the place where his house once stood, a shot was fired, causing Shammaly and other Palestinians and international activists to take momentary shelter in a nearby alley, before returning to search the rubble. Then, at 3:30pm, as he returned to walk and call out the names of his relatives, he unknowingly crossed the death line. At this moment the Golani sniper recognised Salem Khalil Shammaly putting one leg over the death line. In the three independent interviews I conducted, they all brought up Shammaly's green shirt, which drew the attention of both the sniper and the commanding officer in the other house. Shammaly was an easy target because of his brightly coloured shirt.

The sniper announced that someone had crossed the 'death line' and requested permission to shoot. The commanding officer stood over him and ordered him to wait, and then turned off his radio. Only then did he give the permission to shoot once. This shot hit Shammaly on the left side of his body and his left hand, causing him to fall to the ground. The sniper requested permission to finish him off. The officer stood silent for a moment, and then said: 'wait, wait'. He then gave the soldier permission to kill Shammaly. With two additional shots the sniper confirmed his death. The officer then complimented the sniper and turned his radio back on. This is not the only deliberate killing of a Palestinian civilian with impunity that occurred, but it is the only one that was caught on film.

Eran Efrati

What happened in Khuza'a

Testimony of Mohammed Omer

Mohammed Omer is a Palestinian journalist from Rafah refugee camp in Gaza. He writes for The Nation, Al Jazeera, *and* New Statesman, *among many publications. In 2007, he was awarded the Martha Gelhorn Prize for Journalism, and the Ossietzky Prize by Norwegian PEN, in 2009.*

My focus is generally on one of the most hard hit areas, Khuza'a, east of Khan Younis, in the southern Gaza Strip. I was the first to get into Khuza'a during a ceasefire to find massive damage. My contribution focuses on three main cases.

The first is Mohammed Tawfiq Qudeh, a 64-year-old, who used to live in Khuza'a before Israeli troops invaded his area. The Qudeh family was among those survivors I met during the first ceasefire. I have focused my investigations on the execution of Mr. Qudeh. His home had come under constant bombardment, while bulldozers tried to break into one side of his house. Mr. Qudeh told his family he would open the door and talk peacefully with the Israeli soldiers, explaining to them that there were only civilians in the house. He spoke to them in English, Hebrew, Arabic and Spanish. He told his family that using these languages would help to avoid any misunderstandings. He moved closer, speaking softly and politely in all four languages.

'Please don't shoot me,' he said to the Israeli troops.

Suddenly, a muffled shot came from a short, blonde-haired, blue-eyed soldier holding an M-16 in his shaking hands. He was only about 20 years old. Raghad, 20 years old, and Buthina Qudeh, 35 years old, told me the details of what happened to her family. Raghad Qudeh stood outside her uncle's home in Khuza'a where she says an Israeli soldier executed him on 25 July.

The second case is that of Khalil Al-Najjar, the Imam of the mosque of Khuza'a, who was at his brother's home with his mother, siblings, in-laws, and children. There were 15 family members in all. They were under constant Israeli artillery fire all night, not knowing what would happen with each passing second, apart from bombs raining around them.

'A tank shell hit, and there was heavy black smoke in the building, so we ran under the staircase to hide and rest for a few minutes,' Najjar told me. As the bombing continued, automatic gunfire was heard outside. 'We shouted out that we were civilians. But more bullets were fired after we declared ourselves as civilians,' said Najjar who, at 55 years old, is a well-known and highly respected imam in his community.

A few minutes later, a military dog rushed into the house, terrifying the children – the imam shouted out in Hebrew to the soldiers behind a wall riddled with bullet-holes: 'We are civilians, we have children and babies with no medicine or milk.'

The soldiers shouted back, in Hebrew, ordering him and the family to: 'Get out, one by one.'

'In front of all these women, I was forced to undress until I was naked, at gunpoint,' recalls the imam, while walking through the destruction in his neighbourhood. The imam was soon ordered to dress and was ushered outside at gunpoint, along with his brother. Najjar was then told to walk ahead of the soldiers down the centre of the street, while calling on all young residents to come outside and surrender.

The third case is that of Dr. Kamal Qudeh, a doctor serving this small village near Gaza's border with Israel. His story begins when the initial Israeli attack started; when it came, it was unexpected. On 17 July 2014, Israeli F16s dropped leaflets ordering people to leave their homes before a ground offensive started on 20 July.

> 'The day [20 July] came, but all seemed normal in Khuza'a. So people returned, thinking the leaflets had been a false alarm. Then, on 21 July, in the afternoon, an Israeli F16's missile hit the main road connecting Khuza'a with neighbouring villages,' Dr Qudeh told me.

This left him the only doctor in his area who could offer health care. He told me

> 'We had to make a decision to go by ourselves, without protection, and get to the village entrance. There were around 2,000 of us, walking toward Israeli tanks ... I told the Israelis, "We are civilians, unarmed, and we need safe shelter, we have women, children and elderly and we want to evacuate peacefully".'

The Israeli troops replied through loudspeakers that there was no co-ordination and everyone should return home. 'We stayed there, standing, hoping they would have compassion and let us through,' Dr Qudeh said.

While Dr Qudeh was treating victims inside, the outside area of his clinic was hit by two Israeli drone missiles – window glass shattered on those receiving treatment, and scores more people were injured outside.

At this time, his own brother, Ahmed Qudeh, and many family members including his sister sustained injuries. Dr Qudeh himself suffered shrapnel injuries to his leg and arm.

At 6am, Israeli troops fired tear gas, leaving people stunned and in respiratory distress. They had to help each other breathe using mouth-to-mouth resuscitation. At 7am, an Israeli missile hit the basement.

> 'The door was blown off and we had to escape. I shouted out: "All of you, come this way to get out of here, come on!"'

About 2,000 people were outside on the street and were met by Israeli tanks. This time, they were allowed to pass, though only for about 500 metres before being led onto a sandy road full of holes and tracks left by Israeli bulldozers.

> 'The road was covered with cactus thorns and stones crushed by heavy machines, and we were mostly barefoot and naked from top to bottom, showing Israeli troops that we were unarmed and just civilians,' he told me. "We are peaceful men, women and children, young and elderly, who want safety"– this was what we told the Israeli troops.'

Dr Qudeh and others carried some 130 injured people on their shoulders. On the way, an elderly man, Ismail Abu Rejela, was killed by random fire. Other patients were pulled on donkey carts as they made their way to Nasser Hospital, in Khan Younis, about two hours walk to the west.

Mohammed Omer

The world on notice

Ahdaf Soueif

In 2007, Ahdaf Soueif founded Engaged Events, which organises the Palestine Festival of Literature in the cities of occupied Palestine and Gaza. Her bestselling novel, The Map of Love, *has been translated into 30 languages. She writes for* The Guardian *and the Egyptian daily* Al-Shorouk. *This article is a transcription of her comments to the press following the Extraordinary Session on Gaza of the Russell Tribunal on Palestine, held in Brussels in September 2014.*

To be completely blunt, we at the Russell Tribunal are putting the world on notice, that in Gaza we are heading towards crimes of great magnitude. I'm not a lawyer, and I will not quibble about words; I will not quibble about whether we're talking genocide or whether we're talking extermination. We're talking about the likely murder of large numbers of unarmed and captive civilians. Looking at the narrative that has led us to here, and looking at components of the spectacle that we are witnessing, I think that this is an inescapable conclusion. We all know – you all know – that the last aggression on Gaza did not come out of the blue: this is the latest in a series of aggressions that have happened across the last few years, since the siege on Gaza was put in place, if not before.

If we look at the characteristics of this attack: we have an unprecedented level of aggression, we have a captive population that is not allowed to escape, and that does not have safe refuge within the Gaza enclave. We look at the length of the attack and how it was sustained, even in the face of widespread international condemnation. We look at the amount of munitions that were used, and we look at the proportion and the number of civilians, the number of children, the number of families that were wiped out. These are all characteristics that one would have thought would be impossible to get away with, yet Israel is getting away with this attack.

We look at the destruction of healthcare, of infrastructure, of community facilities, of industries, of farmland; we look at a destruction that is meant to last, such as the desertification of land and the diversion of water; we look at long-term consequences. These are all crimes of magnitude. I still find it unbelievable that Israel has actually gotten away with this so far.

The Russell Tribunal would like also to draw attention to evidence that we've heard – it is anecdotal, but it is very telling in the mindsets, the attitudes that it describes – for example, the jokiness with which killing is undertaken. Somebody is asked to step forward, take out his lighter, hold it up, and when he does this he is shot. The game-playing, the imaginary red line that the soldiers draw that nobody else knows about, and when somebody crosses it they get killed. The appearance of randomness; things like: 'Who speaks Hebrew?' – someone steps forward – and gets shot. I think that what all this anecdotal evidence points to is a contempt for the recipients of the violence, and it also – and that is part of the contempt – belittles the experience. It belittles the action. It is as if these actions are not taking place in a serious world, in a world where one is accountable. And that, I believe, is incredibly dangerous. It belittles the people, and it belittles the significance of what is happening to them, it takes the crimes that are being committed against them lightly, and it encourages the world to take them lightly. When we see this in the wider context of the racist attitudes and the racist language that is becoming common in Israel – you saw yesterday the slides that were shown. I will quote only a couple of them, just because they are so incredibly shocking. Here's Naftali Bennett himself:

> 'I've killed many Arabs in my life, and there's no problem with that.'

There were various others:

> 'Let us turn this army into an army of avengers';

> 'Hitler was right but he got the wrong people.'

This is the discourse that is surrounding and that is creating the environment for the actions of the Israeli army in Gaza. So, as I said, we are putting the world on notice that we, with very heavy hearts, believe that something of great magnitude will happen, and we believe that we are in time – the world is in time – to stop it, if the world will take action.

As Michael Mansfield said, we have a list of actions and a list of demands for the international community, for the European Union, for the United Nations, all listed at the end of the summary of findings.

I would like, finally, to make two points. One is that there is no need to speak about the resilience, the *sumoud*, the grace, the courage, the humanity of the Palestinians. We would not all be here were that not something that we know about and that we honour.

We would also like to commend and to honour the small number of Jewish Israelis who are standing against what is happening in their country and in their society. We heard from very brave people yesterday, we hear from brave people all the time really, whether they have had to leave and are living outside, in the international community, or whether they are remaining at great, great cost to themselves and to their families and to their lives within the state of Israel: we honour them and we commend them and we stretch out a hand of friendship and solidarity to them.

Jurors Adhaf Soueif, Richard Falk (on her right), Ken Loach and Vandana Shiva

Gaza under attack

Summary of findings

Russell Tribunal on Palestine

An Extraordinary Session on Gaza of the Russell Tribunal on Palestine took place at the Albert Hall in Brussels, on 25 September 2014. This is the Tribunal's preliminary summary of findings.

'May this tribunal prevent the crime of silence.'

Bertrand Russell, London,
13 November 1966

1. When images of the death, destruction and desperation inflicted on Palestinian citizens of Gaza were broadcast in July and August of 2014, people all over the world were struck with a visceral sense of indignation, anger and disgust. For too long, crimes and serious human rights violations have been committed against the Palestinian people by the occupying Israeli authorities with complete impunity. The occupation, blockade and siege imposed on the territory of Gaza amount to a regime of collective punishment, but the most recent conflict represents a clear intensification of the campaign to collectively punish and terrorise the civilian population. Not only was 'Operation Protective Edge' the third major military assault on Gaza in six years, but it was marked by a significant escalation in the scale, severity and duration of the attack. It was Israel's heaviest assault on the Gaza Strip since the beginning of its occupation of the Palestinian territories in 1967. Given this cyclical and devastating pattern of violence and the likelihood of its continuation, the members of the Tribunal were conscious of the need to give a voice to the people of Gaza and to express the overwhelming need for urgent action. The Russell Tribunal on Palestine hopes to act as a voice of conscience and to contribute some measure of accountability for these appalling and inhumane acts.

2. Over the course of the 50-day conflict,

some 700 tons of ordnance were deployed by the Israeli military forces in the context of a sustained aerial bombardment and ground offensive. This approximate figure equates to the dropping of two tons of ordnance per square kilometre of the Gaza Strip. These actions resulted in: the deaths of 2,188 Palestinians, at least 1,658 of whom were civilians; 11,231 civilians injured; damage to 18,000 housing units (13% of all available housing stock in Gaza was completely or partially destroyed); the internal displacement of some 110,000 civilians; the complete destruction of eight medical facilities and damage to many others, such that 17 out of 32 hospitals were damaged and six closed down as a result; massive destruction of water facilities leaving some 450,000 civilians unable to access municipal water supplies; the destruction of Gaza's only power plant facility rendering the entire Gaza Strip without electricity for approximately 20 hours per day, thereby having a profound impact on water treatment, food supply and the capacity of medical facilities to treat the wounded and displaced; numerous attacks on and destruction of UN sponsored and controlled infrastructure, including three UNRWA schools which were being used as temporary centres of refuge; the total destruction of some 128 businesses and approximately US$550 million worth of damage caused to agricultural land and livestock; attacks on cultural and religious property; and finally, the conflict has left some 373,000 children in need of direct and specialised psychosocial support. The attack was widespread and systematic to the extent that the Palestinian Authority estimates that it will require US$7.8 billion to repair the damage caused to civilian and state infrastructure.

3. The Russell Tribunal on Palestine (RToP) is an international citizen-based Tribunal of conscience, created in response to the demands of civil society (non-governmental organisations, unions, charities, faith-based organisations) to educate public opinion and exert pressure on decision-makers. The RToP is imbued with the same spirit and espouses the same rigorous rules as those inherited from the Tribunal on Vietnam (1966-1967), established by the eminent scholar and philosopher Bertrand Russell. The Tribunal operates as a court of the people, with public international law (including international human rights law, international humanitarian law, and international criminal law) constituting the frame of reference of the Russell Tribunal on Palestine.

4. Following Israel's military operations in the Gaza Strip in July-August 2014, a decision was taken to urgently reconvene the RToP for an

extraordinary session to examine the nature of potential international crimes committed in Gaza. During the course of this extraordinary session the RToP has received testimony from some sixteen individual witnesses providing eyewitness and expert opinion on a range of issues of direct relevance to the events in Gaza in the summer of 2014. The members of the Tribunal jury were moved and deeply disturbed by the harrowing evidence provided by the witnesses. Following the hearings and the deliberations of the jury on 24 September 2014, the findings of the extraordinary session of Russell Tribunal on Palestine are summarised as follows.

The Use of Force

5. Israel is the occupying power in the Gaza Strip. As the occupier, Israel cannot be considered to be acting in self-defence under the rules of public international law in its resort to the use of force in Gaza. Israel did not respond to an armed attack by the military forces of another state; rather it acted as an occupying power using force to effect its control of the occupied territory and its domination over the occupied population. Under international law, people living under colonial rule or foreign occupation are entitled to resist occupation. Israel's actions are those of an occupying power using force to maintain its occupation and to suppress resistance, rather than a state resorting to force in lawful self-defence. The ongoing occupation of Palestinian territories and the permanent blockade of Gaza are themselves acts of aggression as defined by the UN General Assembly in Resolution 3314 (1974) (Art. 3, a and c); the Tribunal notes that an aggressor cannot claim self-defence against the resistance to its aggression. Operation Protective Edge was part of the enforcement of the occupation and ongoing siege of the Gaza Strip. This siege amounts to collective punishment in violation of Article 33 of the Fourth Geneva Convention.

War Crimes

6. The evidence provided by the witnesses who appeared before the RToP covers only a tiny fraction of the incidents that occurred during Operation Protective Edge. Their testimony, however, coupled with the extensive documentation of Israel's attacks in the public realm, leads inescapably to the conclusion that the Israeli military has committed war crimes in the process. Israel's forces have violated the two cardinal principles of international humanitarian law – the need to distinguish clearly between civilian targets and military targets; and the need for the use of military

violence to be proportionate to the aims of the operation. It has done so through the scale of its bombardment of Gaza and its shelling of civilian areas, including hospitals, schools and mosques. An estimated 700 tons of munitions were employed by the Israeli military during the operation, in contrast to 50 tons during Operation Cast Lead in 2008-09. Civilians in Gaza have been terrorised by this bombardment, as well as denied the right to flee the territory to seek protection and assistance as refugees from war in breach of the right to leave one's country pursuant to article 13 (2) of the UN Declaration on Human Rights.

7. Evidence heard by the Tribunal suggests that war crimes committed by Israeli forces include (but are not limited to) the crimes of:
- wilful killing (including summary executions by ground troops and killings of civilians by snipers around houses occupied by Israeli forces inside Gaza);
- extensive destruction of property, not justified by military necessity (including the destruction of essential services, in particular Gaza's only functioning power plant and the apparently systematic targeting of the water and sewage infrastructure);
- intentionally directing attacks against the civilian population and civilian objects (including extensive and wanton artillery shelling and aerial bombardment of densely populated civilian areas);
- intentionally launching attacks in the knowledge that such attacks would cause incidental loss of life or injury to civilians or damage to civilian objects or widespread, long-term and severe damage to the natural environment which would be clearly excessive in relation to the concrete and direct overall military advantage anticipated even when rockets have been launched by Hamas from civilian locations (i.e. the use of disproportionate force, explicitly stated and implemented by the Israeli military in the form of its 'Dahiya doctrine', which involves a policy of deliberately using disproportionate force to punish the civilian population collectively for the acts of resistance groups or political leaders);
- intentionally directing attacks against buildings dedicated to religion or education (including repeatedly and knowingly targeting UN schools operating as places of refuge for civilians);
- intentionally directing attacks against hospitals, medical units and personnel (including the direct shelling of hospitals resulting in the killing and forced evacuation of wounded civilians, as well as apparent patterns of the targeting of visibly marked medical units and ambulance

workers performing their duties);
- utilising the presence of a civilian or other protected person to render certain points, areas or military forces immune from military operations (i.e. the use of Palestinian civilians as human shields);
- employing weapons, projectiles and material and methods of warfare which are of a nature to cause superfluous injury or unnecessary suffering or which are inherently indiscriminate (including flechette shells, DIME weapons, thermobaric munitions ('carpet' bombs), and munitions containing depleted uranium);
- the use of violence to spread terror among the civilian population in violation of the laws and customs of war (including the employment of a 'knock on the roof' policy whereby small bombs are dropped on Palestinian homes as a warning signal in advance of larger bombardments to follow).

8. Allegations of the targeting of civilians and the use of indiscriminate weapons by the Palestinian resistance during Operation Protective Edge have been clearly stated in the public realm by the Israeli authorities. The information available to the Tribunal is that 66 Israeli soldiers and 7 civilians in Israel were killed by Palestinian armed groups during Operation Protective Edge, with 469 soldiers and 837 civilians wounded. There is also, however, contradictory information and unclear statistics from official Israeli sources regarding Palestinian rockets, and Israel's military censor has a gag order in effect, making it extremely difficult to identify where the rockets fell without co-operation from the authorities. The Israeli authorities did not accept the invitation to appear before the Tribunal to state their case. This notwithstanding, the RToP emphasises as a matter of principle that any armed group that directs its firepower at a civilian population thereby violates the laws of war. Where such firing results in the deaths of civilians, war crimes will have potentially been committed by those responsible. Firing weapons which are incapable of making the distinction between military and civilian target is itself criminal.

Crimes against Humanity
The contextual elements of crimes against humanity
9. For an apparently 'ordinary' domestic criminal act to reach the threshold of a crime against humanity, there are certain contextual legal elements that must be satisfied. There must be a widespread or systematic attack against a civilian population, and the acts of the perpetrator must form part

of that attack and be committed with knowledge of the wider context of the attack. Under the Rome Statute of the International Criminal Court, there is an additional legal element to be proven, which is the existence of a State or organisational policy to commit such an attack. Article 7 of the Statute of the International Criminal Court lists several specific crimes against humanity: murder; extermination; enslavement; deportation or forcible transfer of population; imprisonment or other severe deprivation of physical liberty; torture; rape and sexual violence; persecution; enforced disappearance; apartheid; and other inhumane acts. While the Tribunal is confident that findings could be reached under each of these respective headings, given the specific focus of this extraordinary session and the resources available, the RToP limits itself to findings with respect to: (i) murder; (ii) extermination; and (iii) persecution.

10. The preponderance of the evidence received by the RToP clearly establishes that an attack against a civilian population has taken place. The sheer scale of civilian deaths, injuries, and the destruction of civilian housing, provide a clear indication that a prima facie case can be established that Operation Protective Edge was overwhelmingly directed at the civilian population of Gaza.

11. In light of the testimony received and summarised above regarding the extent of the loss of life and destruction of property caused by Israel, considered alongside the data compiled by the various offices of the UN and human rights organisations on the ground, the Tribunal finds that there is compelling evidence establishing a strong prima facie case that the attack against the civilian population of Gaza was widespread and systematic.

12. In relation to the policy requirement, the Tribunal has heard testimony pertaining specifically to three policy directives of the Israeli military – namely, the Dahiya Doctrine (which involves the deliberate use of disproportionate force to collectively punish the civilian population for the acts of resistance groups or political leaders), the Hannibal Directive (the destruction of an entire area for the purpose of preventing the capture of Israeli soldiers) and the Red Line policy (which involves the creation of a 'kill zone' beyond an arbitrary and invisible 'red line' around houses occupied by Israeli forces). Each of these policies deliberately and flagrantly disregards protections afforded to civilians and civilian property under international humanitarian law, and fundamentally involves

indiscriminate violence against the civilian population of Gaza. As such their implementation amounts to a prima facie case of a specific policy on the part of the Government of Israel and the Israeli occupying forces to target civilian areas with disregard for civilian life. The Tribunal finds that there is a compelling case to be made that the contextual elements of crimes against humanity, as outlined above, are satisfied for the purposes of Article 7 of the Statute of the International Criminal Court; specifically with respect to the selected crimes of (i) murder; (ii) extermination; and (iii) persecution.

Murder

13. The crime against humanity of murder requires that the perpetrator kills (or caused the death) of one or more persons. The International Criminal Tribunal for the former Yugoslavia has defined murder as the 'unlawful, intentional killing of a human being'. The RToP finds that a strong prima facie case can be made that a significant proportion of the Palestinian civilian fatalities during Operation Protective Edge were the result of deliberate, unlawful and intentional killings. The RToP has heard testimony relating to a number of individual incidents, such as the deliberate execution of Salem Khalil Shammaly for crossing an imaginary red line while searching for family members in Shuja'iyya and the deeply disturbing circumstances of the killing of 64 year-old Mohammed Tawfiq Qudeh in his own home. The RToP finds that their deaths are prima facie examples of the crime against humanity of murder, in addition to the war crime of wilful killing.

Extermination

14. Under the Statute of the International Criminal Court, the crime of extermination includes both mass killings and the intentional infliction of conditions of life (including depriving access to food, water or medical treatment) calculated to bring about the destruction of part of a population. There is therefore a degree of common ground between the crime against humanity of extermination and the crime of genocide. However, while the crime of extermination frequently involves a large number of victims, it differs from genocide in that it does not require that the victim(s) be part of a protected group, or that the perpetrator had the specific intent to bring about the destruction of the group in whole or in part.

15. During the course of this extraordinary session, the RToP has received detailed and wide-ranging testimony with respect to attacks on civilian

populations and protected civilian property which directly resulted in the mass fatalities. In particular, the Tribunal has received detailed testimony relating to attacks on medical facilities and personnel. The deliberate and indiscriminate targeting of medical infrastructure contributed substantially to the loss of civilian life. Additional deliberate and indiscriminate attacks on civilian infrastructure such as the Gazan power plant also contributed to the increase in the death toll. Coupled with the denial of a humanitarian corridor, the sealing of the Erez and Rafah crossings and the targeting of UNRWA infrastructure, this contributed to the infliction of conditions of life calculated to bring about the destruction of part of the population of Gaza.

Persecution

16. The crime against humanity of persecution involves the intentional and severe deprivation of fundamental human rights against members of a group or collectivity. The group must be targeted for a discriminatory purpose, such as on political, racial, national, ethnic, cultural, gender or religious grounds. This element of discriminatory intent makes the crime of persecution somewhat similar to the crime of genocide, although crucially persecution does not require the establishment of a specific intent to destroy the group in whole or in part. The RToP determines that persecutory acts may be considered under the following three categories of conduct:
- Discriminatory acts causing physical or mental harm;
- Discriminatory infringements on freedom;
- Offences against property for discriminatory purposes.

17. In line with the findings adopted in previous sessions of the RToP and the continuing escalation of violence against the Palestinian people, the Tribunal finds that the actions and policies of the Government of Israel and the Israeli military are inherently discriminatory against the Palestinian people. The Tribunal determines that in its actions and policies the Government of Israel and Israeli military discriminate against the Palestinian people, and in this instance specifically the people of Gaza, on the basis of, inter alia, political affiliation, nationality, ethnicity, religion, culture and gender. The Tribunal finds grounds to believe that a host of additional crimes and violations of fundamental human rights have been and continue to be committed on discriminatory grounds against the Palestinian people and the population of Gaza. In this respect the Tribunal notes the following non-exhaustive list of violations: murder; torture (including the case of 16 year old Ahmad Abu Raida, who was abducted

by the Israeli military, whipped with a wire and threatened with sexual assault while under interrogation, and forced to act as a human shield for the Israelis); sexual violence (such as Khalil Al-Najjar, the imam in Khuza'a, who was forced to strip naked in public); physical violence not constituting torture; cruel and inhumane treatment or subjection to inhumane conditions; constant humiliation and degradation; terrorising the civilian population (including examples of Gazan citizens being instructed by the Israeli military to remain in their homes and then being subjected to bombardment); unlawful arrest and detention; imprisonment or confinement; restrictions on freedom of movement (including the denial of a humanitarian corridor or ability to leave the territory of Gaza); and the confiscation or destruction of private dwellings, businesses, religious buildings, cultural or symbolic buildings or means of subsistence.

Genocide

18. The international crime of genocide relates to any of the following acts committed with intent to destroy, in whole or in part, a national, ethnic, racial or religious group, as such:
- Killing members of the group;
- Causing serious bodily or mental harm to members of the group;
- Deliberately inflicting on the group conditions of life calculated to bring about its physical destruction in whole or in part;
- Imposing measures intended to prevent births within the group;
- Forcibly transferring children of the group to another group.

19. Direct and public incitement to genocide is also an international crime, irrespective of whether anyone acts as a result of the incitement.

20. It is clear that the Palestinians constitute a national group under the definition of genocide. It has been established that Israeli military activities considered under the heads of war crimes and crimes against humanity meet the acts set forth in sub-paragraphs (a) to (c) above.

21. The crime of genocide is closely related to crimes against humanity. Where persecution as a crime against humanity aims to protect specific groups from discrimination, the criminalisation of genocide aims to protect such groups (national, racial, ethnic, religious) from elimination. The sometimes fine distinction between the two crimes, characterised by the 'intent to destroy' element, was explained by the judges at the Yugoslavia Tribunal: 'When persecution escalates to the extreme form of

wilful and deliberate acts designed to destroy a group or part of a group, it can be held that such persecution amounts to genocide.'

22. Israel's policies and practices in Palestine have for decades aimed at ensuring that Palestinians submit to Israeli domination. This has been effected through settler colonial policies based on the displacement and dispossession of Palestinians since the establishment of the state of Israel in 1948. This process continues today through the settlement of the West Bank and imposition of a regime of apartheid and segregation, the siege of Gaza and the prolonged collective punishment of its people, as well as the criminal conduct of repeated military operations and systemic violations of Palestinian human rights designed to ensure that Palestinians forfeit their right to self-determination and continue to leave their country.

23. Throughout that period, Israel's occupation policies appeared to be aimed at the control and subjugation of the Palestinian people, rather than their physical destruction as such. Recent years have seen an upsurge in vigilante style 'price tag' attacks on Palestinian people, homes, and religious sites in the West Bank and Israel. Characterised by racist threats against Palestinians, such rhetoric escalated rapidly and across all forms of media and public discourse in Israel during the summer of 2014. The scale and intensity of Operation Protective Edge indicates an unprecedented escalation of violence against the Palestinian people. For this reason, the RToP is compelled to now, for the first time, give serious examination to Israeli policy in light of the prohibition of genocide in international law.

24. The Tribunal has received evidence demonstrating a vitriolic upswing in racist rhetoric and incitement during the summer of 2014. The evidence shows that such incitement manifested across many levels of Israeli society, on both social and traditional media, from football fans, police officers, media commentators, religious leaders, legislators, and government ministers. This can be understood in varying degrees as incitement to racism, hatred, and violence. The evidence shows that the speech and language used in the summer of 2014 did, on occasion, reach the threshold where it can only be understood as constituting direct and public incitement to genocide.

25. Some of this incitement, in a manner similar to genocidal situations elsewhere, is characterised not only by explicit calls for violence against the target group, but in the employment of sexualised (rape), gendered, and

dehumanising memes, motifs, and prejudices. The RToP heard evidence of multiple examples of such incitement. One notable instance being Israeli legislator Ayelet Shaked's widely reported publication in July 2014 defining 'the entire Palestinian people [as] the enemy', arguing for the destruction of 'its elderly and its women, its cities and its villages, its property and its infrastructure', and stating that the 'mothers of terrorists' should be destroyed, 'as should the physical homes in which they raised the snakes.'

26. The RToP notes that the legal definition of genocide demands proof of a specific intent on the part of the perpetrator not simply to target people belonging to a protected group, but to target them with the intention of destroying the group. It would be for a criminal court to determine whether such specific intent is present in a given situation, on the basis of scrutiny of the relevant evidence for the purposes of prosecution of such crimes. The RToP notes that alternative, broader understandings of genocide beyond that defined for the purposes of individual criminal responsibility have also been suggested as applying to the situation in Gaza. The cumulative effect of the long-standing regime of collective punishment in Gaza appears to inflict conditions of life calculated to bring about the incremental destruction of the Palestinians as a group in Gaza. This process has been exacerbated by the scale of the violence in the Operation Protective Edge, the continuation of the siege of Gaza and the denial of the capacity to rebuild. The Tribunal emphasises the potential for a regime of persecution, such as that demonstrated in section III above, to become genocidal in effect. In light of the clear escalation in the physical and rhetorical violence deployed in respect of Gaza in the summer of 2014, the RToP emphasises the obligation of all state parties to the 1948 Genocide Convention 'to take such action under the Charter of the United Nations as they consider appropriate for the prevention and suppression of acts of genocide'.

27. The prohibition of genocide – and of direct and public incitement to genocide – constitutes a *jus cogens* (non-derogable) norm of international law. According to the 1948 Genocide Convention, individuals who attempt or who incite to genocide 'shall be punished, whether they are constitutionally responsible rulers, public officials or private individuals'. It is thus incumbent on all states to take the appropriate action in line with their legal obligations to investigate and prosecute those responsible for such crimes. It is further incumbent on all states to ensure that the state of Israel does not, through the persons of its military and government, 'engage in conspiracy, incitement, attempt and complicity in genocide'.

28. The evidence received by the Tribunal demonstrates that the state of Israel is failing to respect its obligations to prevent and to punish the crime of direct and public incitement to genocide. This is in keeping with the warning issued by the Special Advisers of the UN Secretary-General on the Prevention of Genocide, and on the Responsibility to Protect, in July 2014, in response to Israel's actions in Palestine: 'We are equally disturbed by the flagrant use of hate speech in the social media, particularly against the Palestinian population'. The Special Advisers noted that individual Israelis had disseminated messages that could be dehumanising to the Palestinians and had called for the killing of members of this group. The Advisers reasserted that incitement to commit atrocity crimes is prohibited under international law.

29. Previous sessions of the RToP have established that the Israeli state is implementing an apartheid system based on the dominance of Israeli Jews over Palestinians. Beyond the prolonged siege and collective punishment of the Palestinians of Gaza, the ongoing settlement project in the West Bank, and the now regular massive military assaults on the civilian population of the Gaza Strip, one must add the increase in aggravated racist hate speech. It is recognised that in a situation where patterns of crimes against humanity are perpetrated with impunity, and where direct and public incitement to genocide is manifest throughout society, it is very conceivable that individuals or the state may choose to exploit these conditions in order to perpetrate the crime of genocide. Alert to the increase in anti-Palestinian speech which constitutes the international crime of direct and public incitement to genocide, and the failure of the Israeli state to fulfil its obligations to prevent and punish incitement to genocide, the RToP is at this time compelled to place the international community on notice as to the risk of the crime of genocide being perpetrated. The jury has listened to alarming evidence over the course of this extraordinary session; we have a genuine fear that in an environment of impunity and an absence of sanction for serious and repeated criminality, the lessons from Rwanda and other mass atrocities may once again go unheeded.

V. Consequences & Action

30. In view of the above findings, the Russell Tribunal on Palestine calls on the state of Israel to immediately:
- end the occupation and respect the Palestinian right to self-determination;
- fully respect its obligations under international law;

- provide full reparations to the victims of human rights violations;
- release all political prisoners;
- genuinely investigate and prosecute any individual suspected of being responsible for international crimes;
- act to prevent and punish any acts in violation of the Convention Against Genocide.

31. To Israel and Egypt:
Immediately lift the siege and blockade of Gaza and permit the unhindered reconstruction of the Gaza Strip as well as permitting unhindered access to media, humanitarian, and human rights organisations.

32. To the European Union:
In line with EU policy on restrictive measures, to pursue the objectives of preserving peace, strengthening international security, developing and consolidating democracy and the rule of law, and respect for human rights and fundamental freedoms, to adopt restrictive measures against Israel, and specifically:
- to suspend the EU-Israel association agreement;
- to suspend the EU-Israel scientific co-operation agreement and to immediately cease co-operation with Israeli military companies;
- to impose a comprehensive arms embargo on Israel, including prohibitions on the sale, supply, transfer or export of arms and related materiel of all types; and the prohibition on the provision of financing and technical assistance, brokering services and other services related to military activities;
- to suspend the import of all military equipment from Israel;
- to actively encourage Israel and Palestine to immediately ratify the Rome Statute in line with EU policy on the International Criminal Court;
- to claim reimbursement for damages to EU and/or member state funded infrastructure destroyed by the Israeli military;
- All EU member states to recognise the state of Palestine;
- To advocate and act for the implementation of the International Court of Justice recommendations in its 2004 Advisory Opinion on the legality of the Wall.

33. To UN member states:
- All states to co-operate to bring to an end the illegal situation arising from Israel's occupation, siege and crimes in the Gaza Strip. In light of the obligation not to render aid or assistance, all states must consider

appropriate measures to exert sufficient pressure on Israel, including the imposition of sanctions, the severing of diplomatic relations collectively through international organisations, or in the absence of consensus, individually by breaking bilateral relations with Israel;
- The UN General Assembly to call for a full arms embargo against the state of Israel;
- All states to fulfil their duty 'to take such action under the Charter of the United Nations as they consider appropriate for the prevention and suppression of acts of genocide' and 'to ensure respect' of the 4 Geneva Conventions (GC, Common Art. 1);
- The United States and member states of the European Union to cease exercising pressure on the Palestinian authorities to refrain from engaging the mechanisms of international justice;
- All parties to co-operate with the UN Human Rights Council Commission of Inquiry and to ensure that the Commission is granted full access to Israel and Gaza for the purposes of its investigations;
- UN human rights mechanisms to investigate the violations of the fundamental freedoms and rights of journalists, media workers, and medical personnel;
- Donor states to undertake a full reconfiguration of the international aid regime in Palestine, such that it ceases to underwrite Israeli occupation and destruction;
- All States to support full realisation of Palestinian self-determination including full Palestinian membership of the UN;
- In light of the Responsibility to Protect doctrine, all states to ensure that in light of the continued denial of Palestinian human rights steps are taken to prevent further atrocities.

34. To the Palestine authorities:
- The state of Palestine to accede without further delay to the Rome Statute of the International Criminal Court;
- Fully co-operate with the Human Rights Council Commission of Inquiry;
- Fully engage the mechanisms of international justice.

35. To Global Civil Society:
- To fully support, develop, and expand the Boycott, Divestment and Sanctions movement;
- To support activism aimed at denying Israeli firms and organisations supporting or profiting from the occupation access to international markets;

- To show solidarity with activists taking action to shut down firms aiding and abetting the commission of crimes against Palestinians such as Elbit Systems in the UK;
- To actively lobby and pressure governments to take immediate action to ensure they are not contributing to Israeli crimes and to ensure they are acting in line with the edicts and principles of international law.

'I wish for you all, each of you, to have your own motive for indignation. This is precious. When something outrages you, then you become militant, strong, and involved.'

Stéphane Hessel

Who started the First World War?

John Gittings

John Gittings' excellent book, The Glorious Art of Peace, *is published by Oxford University Press (see Spokesman 118, 120). He reviews six recent works which offer some answers to an abiding question. They are listed at the end.*

Early in 2014, the BBC along with most other British media decided to anticipate the 100th anniversary of the outbreak of the First World War later in the year by firing its big guns of comment, analysis, documentary and feature programmes in advance. In its online *News Magazine* (12 February 2014), the BBC posed the question: Who Started WW1? to ten leading British scholars. It was a question over which, it said, debate still ranged, citing the recent intervention by the then British education secretary Michael Gove, who had complained of the myth – which he claimed to be propagated by 'left-wing academics' – that the war was a 'series of catastrophic mistakes' *(Daily Mail,* 2 January 2014). Of the ten scholars polled, six gave their opinion that Germany with its ally Austria-Hungary was solely or principally to blame; the other four suggested that responsibility should be much more widely shared. Opinions in the first group included that of John Rohl (University of Sussex) that the war resulted from 'a conspiracy between the governments of Germany and Austria-Hungary' and of Annika Mombauer (Open University) that 'the decision-makers of Austria-Hungary and Germany unleashed a war to preserve and expand their empires', while the military historian Max Hastings said that Germany deserved most responsibility, and that the British had to intervene because a victorious Germany 'would never afterwards have accommodated a Britain which still dominated the oceans and global financial system'. Against these views, Richard Evans (Regius professor of history at Cambridge) cited 'the generally positive attitude of European statesmen towards war, based on notions of honour, expectations of a swift victory, and ideas of Social Darwinism', as a significant factor. Sean McKeekin (Koc University, Istanbul) warned against the temptation 'to seek simple, satisfying answers' and judged that 'all five Great Power belligerents, along with Serbia [complicit in the original assassination of the Arch-Duke Ferdinand at Sarajevo] unleashed Armageddon'.

The six books under review here tip the balance more firmly towards the view that all the parties involved shared responsibility, with the exception of the work by Max Hastings. My own reading leads me to believe that this view represents the prevailing academic consensus today. (Regrettably, however, it seems that among the general public, the 'Germany to blame' thesis, which has been propagated by the BBC and other media, is much more widespread.) Three of these six books look at the origins of the war from a broad chronological and thematic perspective (Clark, Hastings, MacMillan), while the other three focus on the events in the immediate month or weeks before its outbreak (Martel, McMeekin, Newton). Both approaches seem to me equally valid and necessary to reach a full understanding. The perennial question 'Who Started the War?' requires a minute examination of the chain of events and decisions in those 30 days between the assassination on 28 June at Sarajevo and the first shot being fired on 28 July by Austro-Hungarian forces. (With typical insularity, British accounts often imply that the war began on 4 August when Britain declared war on Germany – hence the title '37 Days' of a successful BBC feature film shown in the anniversary year.) The larger and more interesting question of 'What Caused the War?' requires us to delve deeply into diplomatic military and political history over at least the previous decade and to look at subjective moods and assumptions among leaders, elites and public opinion in all the countries concerned. It is an immensely rich though difficult subject: these six books alone contain well over three thousand pages of text, apart from footnotes etc, but almost every page is worth reading.

By concluding that the responsibility for the start of World War One was shared by all participants, we are in effect asserting that a tragedy on this scale has a cast of tens if not hundreds of principal actors who between them have staged the play, and that it makes little or no sense to ask 'who is to blame?' Clark in his conclusion to *The Sleepwalkers* puts this very well. The problem with a blame-centred account is not just that one may blame the wrong party, but that it narrows the field of enquiry 'by focusing on the political temperament and initiatives of one particular state rather than on multilateral processes of interaction'. This approach also assumes that decision-makers always make coherent decisions and is likely to lead to the making of 'conspiratorial narratives'. 'The outbreak of war in 1914,' Clark concludes, 'is not an Agatha Christie drama at the end of which we will discover the culprit standing over a corpse in the conservatory with a smoking pistol.'

Besides, we should be clear that the question 'who started it?' is by no means the same as the much broader enquiry as to 'what caused it?' MacMillan's clear summary of the multiple factors which we need to consider is worth quoting at length:

> For a start the arms race, rigid military plans, economic rivalry, trade wars, imperialism with its scramble for colonies, or the alliance systems dividing Europe into unfriendly camps. Ideas and emotions often crossed national boundaries: nationalism with its unsavoury riders of hatred and contempt for others; fears, of loss or revolution, of terrorists and anarchists; hopes, for change or a better world; the demands of honour and manliness which meant not backing down or appearing weak; or Social Darwinism which ranked human societies as if they were species and which promoted a faith not merely in evolution and progress but in the inevitability of struggle. And what about the role of individual nations and their motivations: the ambitions of the rising ones such as Germany or Japan; the fears of declining ones such as Great Britain; revenge for France and Russia; or the struggle for survival for Austria-Hungary?

Yet our enquiry should still begin with the narrow focus implied in the first question before broadening out to examine the underlying causes: the issue of culpability has to be addressed simply because it is the one to which so much commentary has reduced what is a far more complex subject. This is particularly true in these centenary years when, in Britain at least, this reductionism has already assumed such proportions. Far more people will have heard Jeremy Paxman, the spiky BBC interviewer, declare (in his TV series 'Britain's Great War') that 'Kaiser Wilhelm aimed to dominate all of Europe by invading both France and Russia. He also had his eyes on a chunk of the British empire' than will have read – in any one of these books – how the Kaiser hesitated, agonised, and at least twice seized on a hint of possible peace to hold back his generals.

This reductionism is also encountered among some other academics who appear to relish the chance to demolish what they regard as 'myths' about the war, and particularly the 'myth' that everyone shared the blame. Max Hastings, the only representative of this school here – I have included him not only for balance but because his book has other merits – even refers to those holding a different view as 'apologists' for Germany, and he derides what he calls the 'Blackadder take on history'. (This satirical TV series was also blamed by Michael Gove in his egregious *Daily Mail* rant for portraying the war as 'a series of catastrophic mistakes perpetrated by an out-of-touch elite'. Gove also targeted the malign influence of the musical *Oh What a Lovely War*, staged famously by Joan Littlewood in 1964 and later made into a film by Richard Attenborough.)

This hard-headed approach of Hastings and others, I would suggest, is part of a broader neo-revisionist tendency in the post-Cold War climate of Western scholarship to expose such alleged leftwing myths as the contention that the West shared responsibility for the Cold War itself. Douglas Newton sets out in *The Darkest Days* to confront what he calls the 'comforting consensus' that Britain was wholly in the right to go to war and had done everything possible to avoid it. Newton's close examination of the lead-up to the British entry to the war focuses principally on the discussions within the Liberal cabinet under Prime Minister Herbert Asquith, but also takes into full account public opinion and outside political pressures for and against war. In doing so, Newton explicitly targets what he calls the 'feel-good story' that Britain did its very best to avoid war and was driven to intervene only out of 'dire necessity' when Germany finally invaded Belgium. While the timescale of Newton's enquiry is the shortest of the books under review, its implications carry just as far.

Newton's approach is by no means crudely revisionist: he is not recasting Britain as the villain of the piece, but he does seek to show that Britain suffered from many of the same destructive forces in its political culture – and feebleness of leadership – as did the other European players. 'Britain was not especially to blame – but neither was she free from blame – when in 1914 the tragedy of war engulfed a rotten system.' In Newton's version of events, buttressed by a mass of detailed evidence, Britain failed to mediate effectively as a genuinely neutral power and was entrammelled by a perceived need to show solidarity with its Entente partners, Russia and France, whom Britain did little or nothing to restrain.

Clark also sees the British position (or that of the pro-war leadership which prevailed) in similar terms, writing that

> 'Britain accepted – or at least did not challenge – the legitimacy of a Russian strike against Austria to resolve an Austro-Serbian quarrel, and the inevitability of French support for the Russian initiative. The precise circumstances of the Austro-Serbian dispute and questions of culpability were matters of subordinate interest …'

We should not forget that if we wind back the clock to the early days of the July crisis, the threat of war was that of a war between Austria-Hungary and Serbia, the former bent on revenge for the assassination of the Archduke. (We might compare the determination of the US to revenge itself on Afghanistan's Taliban government after 9-11.) Russia was not obliged to intervene. When Russia mobilised and Germany stepped up its own preparations for war, the threat of war was between Russia and Serbia on the one side and Austria-Hungary and Germany on the other. France was not obliged to intervene and could have avoided entanglement by declaring its own neutrality. When it was clear that France and Germany would also go to war, Britain still had the option of neutrality – as was urged by a large body of political and public opinion. Newton's view is not based on the benefit of hindsight but was expressed by critics at the time such as the *Manchester Guardian*. After war was declared between Austria and Serbia, the paper consistently warned against the knock-on dangers of Russia joining the conflict, and denounced the pro-Russian sentiment in the Northcliffe press. On 30 July, the paper criticised Grey and Asquith for having spoken so briefly on the crisis in the House of Commons: 'Sir Edward Grey walks deliberately past opportunities for saying that we are and will be neutral in the quarrels of Europe'. The following day, the *Guardian* expressed its fears that there were secret commitments which would lead Britain to 'the ruinous madness of a share in the wicked gamble of a war between two militarist leagues on the Continent'.

Newton argues powerfully that the '"pro-Entente" interventionists' in the Cabinet, who included the Prime Minister and, with some waverings, Foreign Secretary Edward Grey, steered what was a pro-neutralist majority in the Cabinet towards war, frustrating their demand for a 'credible, active diplomacy of mediation'. Fatally, the neutralists were jockeyed into what amounted to a choice for war on 2 August – in the shape of a pledge of naval assistance to France – *before* news of the German ultimatum to Belgium. Throughout the crisis Asquith and the cabinet as a whole were under pressure from the Conservative party, who 'stood firm for intervention, with no distinction between a war in the east and the west', and from the supporting clamour of the Tory press which called for immediate mobilisation. The navy minister Winston Churchill, although a member of the government, was regarded by the Tories as 'their man in the Liberal Cabinet'. More than once he acted without Cabinet authorisation, in particular on 28 July when he encouraged hard-liners by publicly ordering the British Fleet to be concentrated ready for deployment. Powerful voices in the Foreign Office and the military as well had 'urged British military intervention from the very first days of the crisis'. Domestic politics were also a hidden factor: there was an implicit, and sometimes explicit, threat that if the Cabinet neutralists resigned en masse, the Government would fall or be forced to go into coalition with the pro-war Tories, anyhow.

Newton's emphasis on the strength (but ultimate weakness) of anti-war opinion in the run-up to 4 August is shared by other writers, again reminding us that it is not naïve leftwing revisionism to believe that other choices were available. These sentiments should be seen in the context of the strong current of pro-peace public opinion in many European countries in the late 19th century and the first decade of the 20th. Though the term 'pacifist' was coined at this time to describe such arguments (in a rather more limited sense than it later acquired), they were based on a clear realisation that modern technology and organisation meant that any major war would be a disaster for the winners as well the losers. Martel, in his wide-ranging prologue to *The Month that Changed the World,* sets this out in detail, quoting from hugely popular books such as Norman Angell's *The Great Illusion* and Ivan Bloch's *Is War Now Impossible?* War could no longer be considered a rational policy, Bloch argued: the consequences of war in future would be 'not fighting, but famine, not the slaying of men, but the bankruptcy of nations and the breakup of the whole social organisation'.

And when the war did break out, thoughtful opinion in many quarters knew full well that the prospect was appalling. Max Hastings (who, when not arguing polemically the case for German blame, offers some useful insights) quotes *The Economist.* It warned that 'Since last week millions of men have been drawn from the field and the factory to slay one another by order of the warlords of Europe. It is perhaps the greatest tragedy of human history', and predicted 'a social upheaval, a tremendous upheaval [as] the certain consequence'. The legend that Europe welcomed the conflict, Hastings concludes, 'is today heavily qualified, if not discredited'. In Germany, as MacMillan records, working-class sentiment against war was strong and three quarters of a million marched in demonstrations for peace during the week before the war broke out. Newton gives a vivid account of the huge anti-war demonstration in Trafalgar Square on Sunday 2 August – an event which for readers today evokes more recent scenes of protest there.

> Photographic evidence shows that the crowd was a mixture of middle-class and working-class men and women, with some children too. The hats worn advertised the broad alliance of classes: straw hats, boaters, bowlers, soft hats, and cloth caps. The speakers crowded together on their plinths, flanked by the great bronze lions, under ominously darkening skies. A thunderstorm was brewing.

The demonstrations were meant to be the first in a series and brought together both radicals and socialists, as did similar events around the country. Newton believes that if the neutralist forces had been given more time there was potentially a deep well of public support on which to draw. The movement for neutrality, he writes, was not a last-minute surge of anti-war sentiment, but was based on years of warning by Radical and Labour critics 'against the danger of Britain's entanglement in war by secret diplomacy'.

When we consider both the long-term argument for peace, as it had developed in the peace societies from the mid-19th century onwards, leading to two international peace conferences at The Hague, and the first agreement for arbitration of disputes between states, coupled with the more immediate and widespread opposition to a European war and fears of its terrible consequences, we may reasonably wonder why Europe's leaders did not back off in the summer of 1914. MacMillan puts the issue very well. Very little in history is inevitable, she writes, and European leaders had choices to make: a general war 'could have been avoided up to the last moment on 4 August when the British finally decided to come in'. As well as factors pushing Europe towards war there are other factors, which we should not neglect, pulling towards peace. Perhaps the real question to be asked, MacMillan suggests, is not why did the war break out, but why did the peace not continue, 'why did the forces pushing towards peace – and they were strong ones – not prevail?'

There is a striking degree of consensus today on the issues raised by this enquiry. Most academic opinion (excepting Hastings in this selection) has moved away from the unicausal explanation – Germany was to blame – associated in modern scholarship with the work of Fritz Fischer which dominated the debate in the 1960s and '70s. The result of this, McMeekin observes, had been that 'many historians nearly forgot about the other powers in their zeal to unearth evidence of plotting in Berlin'. (Fischer himself, as Newton points out, 'did not imagine that those in the Kaiser's circle were solely to blame for the European catastrophe'.) We have also moved on from the A J P Taylor thesis – again often simplified at second hand – that, ultimately, the war was caused by the inflexibility of timetables for military mobilisation once they had been set in motion.

Individuals did matter. 'It was Europe's and the world's tragedy,' writes MacMillan, 'that none of the key players in 1914 were great and imaginative leaders who had the courage to stand out against the pressures building up for war.' The three imperial cousins of Britain, Germany and Russia played their solo unhelpful parts: all, writes Hastings, were 'wild cards in the doom game' – although the Kaiser was the wildest of all. MacMillan deplores 'a failure of imagination in not seeing how destructive such a conflict would be and second, their lack of courage to stand up to those who said there was no choice left but to go to war'. Martel shows that as late as 28 July, the major powers were 'extraordinarily close to peace', but the chance was missed. The Russian mobilisation tipped the balance of argument in Berlin towards war. In Britain, the neutralists in the cabinet hesitated to force a political crisis by publicly resigning. Martel argues strongly against the pre-determinist approach of some historians. War was not inevitable, he insists. 'It was the choices that men made during those fateful days that plunged the world into a war.'

Clark devotes a significant section of his book to 'the many voices of European policy-making', asking who governed in each country and how the balance lay between hawks and doves, soldiers and civilians. In another recent book which deserves reading (*The Lost History of 1914: How the Great War Was Not Inevitable*) Jack Beatty argues that personalities and what happened to them could be 'history changing'. If, for example, the wife of France's Minister of Finance, Madame Caillaux, had not caused a national scandal by shooting dead the editor of *Le Figaro* in March 1914, Joseph Caillaux would have become premier in July and his foreign minister would have been the socialist and passionate anti-militarist Jean Jaurès. Historical inevitability, says Beatty, 'is a doctrine for history without people'. Finally, and still controversially, if Lloyd George had remained in the neutralist (and until the end majority) faction within the British cabinet, a very different decision might have been made on 4 August. Chance played a part in other ways, too. After all, as MacMillan writes, 'during previous crises, some as bad as the one of 1914, Europe had not gone over the edge'. If Austria this time had taken punitive action against Serbia within days instead of dithering for weeks, Russia might not have widened the war and the German hawks would have not had time to manoeuvre for a wider war. Even at the last moment, Clark suggests, if the German army had simply 'barged through the south of Belgium', instead of issuing an ultimatum to Brussels which was bound to lead to rejection and resistance, the issue of 'gallant little Belgium' would have had less influence.

The contention for imperial power is also seen as a primary source of de-stabilisation in the long run-up to the war, and particularly in fuelling German resentment. Clark describes this very well: British policy-makers 'proceeded from the assumption that whereas British imperial interests were 'vital' and 'essential', German ones were a mere 'luxury', the energetic pursuit of which must be construed as a provocation by other powers'. Germany by contrast 'showed both the insecurities and the ambitions of a rising world power'. Whenever Germany tried to take territory overseas, MacMillan notes, 'Britain invariably appeared to raise objections'. As Hastings puts it, 'Only Britain and France favoured maintenance of the status quo abroad, because their own imperial ambitions were sated. Others chafed.'

Altough the great alliance blocs seemed solid by the time of the war, their formation had been arbitrary and might well have assumed a different shape. During the decade 1894-1905, Clark observes, it was Russia rather than Germany that posed the most significant long-term threat to British interests, and the Anglo-Russian Convention of 1907 was driven not by hostility to Germany, but by the perceived need to tame the traditional Russian foe. 'Allegiances were not set in stone', writes Hastings, 'they wavered, flickered, shifted.' Britain in 1905 still had contingency plans to fight France, and in 1912 Austria toyed with the idea of a rapprochement with Russia.

We are also reminded that an appetite for war and the hysteria which it could arouse lay not far below the surface of the generally harmonious European power system. MacMillan recalls headlines in the French press during the 1898 Fashoda crisis: 'No Surrender to England', and there was talk on both sides of the Channel about the possibility of war. In the Dogger Bank incident of 1904 when the Russian fleet mistakenly fired on some British fishing boats, the British foreign secretary warned that 'we might find ourselves at war before the week was over'. Clark tells us that the Agadir crisis of 1911 'was allowed to escalate to the point where it seemed that a western-European war was imminent'. Less observed in the same year, Clark notes that Italy's unprovoked war of conquest in Libya (driven by imperialist appetite pure and simple) triggered 'a chain of opportunist assaults on Ottoman territories across the Balkans' which both de-stabilised and focused attention of both power blocs on a region which till then had seemed of secondary interest, with fatal consequences three years later.

Germany's challenge to British naval supremacy, often presented as evidence of a singular expansionist ambition, is also put into more rational context. The Germans, writes Clark, 'had ample reason to believe that they would not be taken seriously unless they acquired a credible naval weapon'. In the end, Germany 'lost the naval race hands down' in part because it slowed down the dreadnought-building programme, as McMeekin observes, in order not to over-antagonise Britain. According to

MacMillan, 'in the two decades before 1914, overall defence spending took up approximately 40 per cent of the British government expenditure, a higher proportion than in any other of the great powers ...' However, there is no doubt that the alleged threat of Germany's naval challenge (we may compare the various Soviet 'missile threats' of the Cold War) contributed to a rise of anti-German hostility in Britain where naval equality would never be tolerated. If Germany secured an Atlantic port at Agadir, Lloyd George warned during that crisis, Britain would face the surrender of its 'international pre-eminence', and 'peace at that price would be a humiliation intolerable for a great nation like ours to endure'.

There is consensus, too, that the Russian preparations to mobilise in the last week of July were crucial in ensuring that 'the looming conflict would not be confined to the Balkans' (Hastings), and that the order for full mobilisation was 'the decision for European war' (McMeekin). It might have been unpalatable for Russia to stand by and watch Austria crush Serbia, but that would surely have been preferable to stoking a European war of whose terrible consequences the wavering Tsar Nicholas was well aware. The fact that Germany would subsequently use the fact of prior Russian mobilisation to justify all the war measures that it then took does not detract from this reality.

Indeed, the principal actors appear to have already lost a sense of perspective in the critical month leading up to the war's outbreak. 'As the great alliance blocs prepared for war', Clark observes, 'the intricate chain of events that had sparked the conflagration was swiftly lost from view.' It was remembered only by a few voices persisting in the argument for peace, while patriotism, spontaneous or forced, dominated the popular discourse in all the combatant countries. More insidiously, it was argued then and still is today that even if other choices and decisions could have been made which might have averted this war, it would have made little difference. Sooner or later, it is claimed, Germany was bound to come into conflict with those European powers who opposed its expansionist designs. This over-determinist approach seeks to render irrelevant the 'what if' or counter-factual questions which we can usefully ask. (What if, asks Newton, Grey had 'put both the Russian and French ambassadors in London under real pressure on the issue of Russia's early mobilisation?') Yet the view that German militarism would have provoked a European war at a later date is open to challenge. As McMeekin argues, Moltke and his fellow military hawks 'had pushed for such a war before 1914, too, without success. Moltke was not sovereign of Germany; he was not even her chancellor.' The truth is that we just do not know how things might have turned out otherwise in the absence of war, but we are entitled to suspect that the outcome could hardly have been worse and in all likelihood would have been a very greater deal better.

What we do know, concludes Martel, 'is how those in positions of authority made the choices that produced unprecedented suffering and upheaval. The tragic era that followed can be explained only by their hubris, combined with chance and circumstance.' Perhaps the most fatal flaw was the conviction of all the leadership elites that 'they could not appear to be weak in the eyes of the others'. Newton's verdict is more trenchant: 'the descent into war revealed the ignominious collapse of essential elements of the old order'. Whatever our conclusion, in the year 2014 we should surely heed MacMillan's warning:

> 'It is easy to throw up one's hands and say the Great War was inevitable but that is dangerous thinking, especially in a time like our own which in some ways, not all, resembles that vanished world of the years before 1914.'

* * *

Christopher Clark, *The Sleepwalkers: How Europe Went to War in 1914,* Penguin, 2013, 736 pages, ISBN 9780141027821, paperback, £10.99; Max Hastings, *Catastrophe: Europe Goes to War, 1914,* Collins, 2014, 672 pages, ISBN 9780007519743, paperback, £9.99; Margaret Macmillan, *The War that Ended Peace: How Europe abandoned peace for the First World War*, Profile, 2014, 704 pages, ISBN 9781846682735, paperback, £9.99; Gordon Martel, *The Month that Changed the World, July 1914,* OUP, 2014, 484 pages, ISBN: 9780199665389, hardback, £22; Sean McMeekin, *July 1914: Countdown to War*, Ikon Books, 2014, 560 pages, ISBN: 9781848316577, paperback, £9.99; Douglas Newton, *The Darkest Days: The Truth behind Britain's Rush to War, 1914*, Verso, 2014, 386 pages, ISBN 9781781683607, hardback, £20.

A Pacifist at War

Bertrand Russell

Bertrand Russell opposed the First World War at its sudden outbreak in August 1914. His opposition was to cost him dear during the difficult years that followed. Russell tells the story of his turbulent war, personal and public, in a selection of his letters and writings from these years, **A Pacifist at War** *(Spokesman £9.99), edited by Nicholas Griffin of McMaster University in Canada, which holds Russell's extensive Archives. In this excerpt, writing to his erstwhile lover Ottoline Morrell in June 1917, Russell recounts his visit to Leeds to celebrate the revolutionary changes taking place in Russia. The February Revolution had removed Tsar Nicholas II, the Provisional Government had been installed, and the October Revolution was still to come. By this stage in the war, Russell had growing doubts about the usefulness of his continuing work for the No-Conscription Fellowship (NCF), which campaigned on behalf of thousands of conscientious objectors (COs) and others who were often brutally mistreated. Catherine Marshall struggled to maintain the NCF. The term 'absolutist' refers to imprisoned conscientious objectors who objected to any work or alternative service that would benefit the war effort. Professor Griffin sets the scene.*

On 3 June 1917, a second mass meeting to welcome the Russian revolution was to be held at Leeds, organised by the Labour movement. Russell travelled to Leeds with Constance and Miles Malleson, Ramsey MacDonald and other Labour leaders. Russell was not among the platform speakers at Leeds, but he spoke from the floor in support of a civil liberties motion along the lines of the 'Charter of Freedom', and received a huge ovation. Three other motions were passed: one welcoming the Russian revolution; one urging peace without annexations or indemnities; and the last, the most radical of all, calling for the formation of workers' and soldiers' councils throughout Britain. Quite how radical this motion was proved a matter of some dispute. W C Anderson of the Independent Labour Party (ILP – the only political party which opposed the war), who moved it, said it was not intended to be subversive; Robert Williams of the Transport Workers' Union, who seconded it, said it meant socialist revolution. Russell was evidently more impressed by Williams. But what quite rightly worried him, despite the euphoria of the meeting, was the weakness of the provisional committee that was set up to implement the fourth resolution. The lack of follow-up doomed any hope of a revolutionary peace in Britain.

[To Ottoline Morrell] **[57 Gordon Sq.]**
5 June 1917

My Darling

I got back from Leeds yesterday. It was a wonderful occasion, but a little disappointing from the point of view of practical outcomes. Snowden and MacDonald and Anderson are not the right men[1] – they have not the sense for swift dramatic action. The right man would be Williams (of the Transport Workers), but he is not yet sufficiently prominent. Smillie is perfect except that he is old. The enthusiasm and all-but unanimity were wonderful – out of 2500, there were only about three dissentients. Nothing was lacking except leaders.

To my great surprise, they gave me about the greatest ovation that was given to anybody. I got up to speak, and they shouted for me to go on the platform, and when I got there they cheered endlessly. They applauded everything that had to do with C.O.'s – Allen's name came up often, and always produced a great cheer.

It was a good beginning, but a very great deal remains to be done. MacDonald, whom I travelled down with, was persuaded we should be broken up by soldiers – he has lost his nerve – he does the things, but expects disaster.

The decision of the French Chamber today is bad.[2] But I feel almost sure peace will come in the autumn.

---

1 All three were parliamentary constitutionalists.
2 Amid strikes and mutinies the French Chamber of Deputies had met in secret session to discuss Franco-Russian relations and French war aims. The socialist deputies had tried to pass a resolution calling, among other things, for peace without annexations or indemnities. In the end, however, the Chamber declared, by 453 votes to 55, its confidence in the government's ability to achieve the restitution of Alsace-Lorraine, the destruction of Prussian militarism, and the imposition of a war indemnity on Germany.

I find it hard to think of anything else. Poor Miss Marshall was there, her mind filled with niggly details of business – she seemed terribly out of place. She has gone away for a holiday now, so I can't get a holiday till August – but her absence is in itself a holiday. I wish I could come to Garsington but I don't know when I can. I go to Manchester this week-end for three meetings – otherwise I shall be here. Goodbye.
Your
B.

Events in Russia further weakened Russell's belief in the usefulness of the NCF. In May he had gone so far as to draft a letter of resignation from his post as acting chairman in which he had explained his doubts:

> Opposition to the government is likely to be strengthened, not so much by pacifist arguments as by economic considerations and resentment at interference with industrial freedom. It is difficult for the N.C.F. as an organization to take any part in such movements, which nevertheless are more likely than direct pacifist efforts to prove effective in moving the world in the direction in which we wish to see it move.
>
> (*Papers*, vol. xiv, p. 163)

Although he did not submit his resignation, the sense that the NCF had ceased to be effective in either its immediate practical aims or in its long-term political ones dogged him through the rest of the year.

With time it had become easy for the government to ignore the lobbying of the NCF on behalf of COs. But then, in 1917, the absolutists found a most improbable ally. Margaret Hobhouse was a pro-war Conservative with close links to Lord Milner in the War Cabinet. Her son, Stephen (Milner's godchild), having become a Quaker, was jailed in 1916 as an absolutist. But this did not change her opinion of the war: in a note left among his papers, Russell said that her son 'persuaded her that Christianity and war were incompatible, so she gave up Christianity.' Her son's plight did, however, persuade her that the COs were being brutally and unjustly treated and she launched a campaign on their behalf. She took her concerns to Milner and he took them to the War Cabinet. From this stage on the NCF was surreptiously involved, providing both Milner and Hobhouse with information. Milner seems to have been quickly persuaded that the COs were being badly treated, but Hobhouse felt he was unlikely to get far with the War Cabinet unless his concerns were backed up by a public campaign. This she proceeded to organize, again seeking the advice of the NCF. Her public campaign was centred round a small book about the COs, '*I Appeal Unto Caesar*', which was published over her name, although it was in fact written by Russell. Russell's authorship was a closely guarded secret: any suggestion he was involved would have undermined the book's effect. There are a few letters from Hobhouse to Russell among Russell's papers and a copy of the following letter to her. She probably destroyed the original, and Russell's other letters, to keep the secret of the book's authorship safe. '*I Appeal Unto Caesar*' was a remarkable success. It sold widely and received favourable notices from papers that would have excoriated anything bearing Russell's name. More importantly, it had a perceptible effect in softening the government's treatment of COs.

[To Margaret Hobhouse]   57 Gordon Square
6 June 1917

Dear Mrs. Hobhouse,

Your letter of the 4th June reached me yesterday. I did not suppose that the Quaker booklet would be of much use for public distribution, but the statistics at the end are useful. I quite agree with you that we cannot expect sympathy for the Tolstoyian [*sic*.] view of life, but the thing that we have to preach is that men ought not to be imprisoned for their opinions even if those opinions are such as most people think harmful.

I feel also a certain scruple in agitating for the release of these men without letting it be known what it is that they really believe. They care more about their beliefs than about themselves, and they think, rightly or wrongly, that they help the spread of their beliefs by being in prison for them. It is hardly fair to them, or even really kind, to minimise in any way their opposition to the views of the majority of mankind. I feel sure this is what your son himself would think.

As you say, the War Office is playing the very game of the men it is persecuting. This fact leads many of them and their friends to deprecate all attempts at securing their release. I do not myself take this view because I care about the conduct of the nation and not only about the C.O.s. But I think that we as well as the authorities realise that a large proportion of the men in prison and of their sympathisers outside dread nothing so much as release because they realise the immense propaganda value of their continued imprisonment. The I.L.P. has done everything it could. Its power is very limited. It was not the I.L.P. but the Trade Unions which secured amnesty at the point of the bayonet.[1]

---

1 In May there had been a wave of strikes in the munitions industries which had forced Lloyd George to launch an inquiry into their causes.

With regard to your letter of June 2. I have the pamphlet well in hand, and I think I quite understand the sort of thing you wish it to be. It will, of course, not be published by the N.C.F. since if it were it could not have the tone that you desire. I thought of making it an expansion of the previous memorandum, less official and more human in its tone, but preserving the same kind of moderation.

With regard to prison reform, I must say that I think Mr. Philip Kerr[1] is deliberately trying to divert you into a direction in which your efforts will be enormously less useful to the C.O.s. I am whole heartedly in favour of agitation for prison reform, but those who hold that the C.O.s ought not to be in prison at all do not wish this question mixed up with the quite different question of the more enlightened treatment of ordinary criminals.

I think you would do well to induce the societies for prison reform to move in that matter, but to keep that quite distinct from the question of the liberation of C.O.s. That agitation ought to be conducted by different people and different methods. Mr. Kerr's proposal seems to me intended to produce delay and to damp down an awkward agitation. I very earnestly hope that you will not fall in with it. But I am proposing to include in the pamphlet an account of prison conditions both in England and Scotland, and this will, I hope, help you in any agitation for prison reform that you may undertake.

My own view is that the prospect of securing unconditional release for the Absolutists within the next few months is very good. I think the whole tone of the world is changing so fast in the direction of greater liberality that it will soon become impossible for the Government to persist in the persecution of opinion. I do not wish to jeopardise the prospect of unconditional release by any agitation calculated to suggest that mere mitigation of punishment might be regarded as satisfactory.

I return Mr. Clark's letter.[2] The point of view expressed in it is that taken by most Quakers. I am grateful to you for letting me see it.

I hope to get the pamphlet finished early next week, and will send it to you as soon as it is typed. If you wish it to be in any definite way different from what I suggested, I should be glad to know.

Yours very truly,
Bertrand Russell

---

1 One of Lloyd George's private secretaries who was gathering information about the COs with a view to making recommendations on their treatment.
2 The letter is lost. Mr Clark was probably Roderic Clark of the Friends' Service Committee.

Though Bertie continued to visit Garsington, his relations with Ottoline became more and more strained. During a visit in late July there was clearly some mutual recrimination; it was perhaps the first time they had both recognized to each other that they were no longer in love. Characteristically, Bertie felt depressed and guilty about it when he got back to London.

[To Ottoline Morrell] [57 Gordon Sq.]
27 July 1917

I wrote you a horrible letter the other day. Today I will try to write more sincerely.

Everything that I do and feel now-a-days is the outcome of despair. Absolutely my whole being went into my love for you, but that turned to despair. I lost the belief that I could do any more philosophy, chiefly through Wittgenstein, and I lost the wish to do it through the war. The war at first raised hopes of new work in me – when I wrote *Social Reconstruction* I was full of hope. Then I realized that I had been much too optimistic about human nature. I have come to hate human life and to have hardly any belief in its possibilities. The work I do is insincere, because it expresses hopes that I really think delusive. I feel dimly that if I made a great enough effort I could find something to live for, but instinctively I put it off till after the war, because I don't want to yield to my mood and give up peace-work; and also because I am so weary that I can't think sanely. I have no real hold on life. I simply don't know how to express the utter devastation inside me. I feel that I am rotting away inwardly. The walls stand for the present, but they must fall sooner or later. The sort of thing you and I had in common depended upon faith and hope, but now I have neither. I used to want to express pain when it had not gone so deep. Now I have no impulse to say anything sincere, and I am only writing this because you wanted me to say what was going on in my mind. I used to hope you could help me to overcome the fundamental despair, but gradually I found you couldn't. I don't regard it as a revelation of the truth of the world, but merely as a morbid state I have got into. There is no cure for it except rest. But unfortunately I can't rest with you, because I can't be superficial with you. I don't think any good is done by expressing a despair which goes as deep as mine does, but my only way of not expressing it is to talk about things that don't go deep. I am profoundly dissatisfied with myself. I should like to live an austere self-reliant life, but I shirk the pain of it. I should not if I had any clear belief, or anything that I felt I could do. Meanwhile I long for death with the same kind of intensity with which I long for the end of the war.

Pain that goes beyond a certain point isolates one, because one cannot escape from it through sympathy. My whole nature has wanted you and cried out to you, but in vain – you thought you could give the sort of response I ought to want, but it was not the sort I really did want. I feel entirely without hope as regards myself. I shall go on being undermined by pain until everything crumbles. The only problem is to put it off as long as possible.

Six months ago I started to write out what I felt, hoping to find some way out. But I broke off in the middle, because it was clear there was no way out. I send you the stuff I wrote – you can throw it away.[1]

The whole trouble is lack of courage. I ought not to care how much I suffer. But things are really dreadful. These days the pavements have been chalked by the newspapers with the notice 'Kerensky shoots traitors' – all London has been gloating and hugging itself with voluptuous delight because Russian regiments that will not fight are being butchered.[2] How is one to bear such a world? I feel an alien, a being from another planet. Each fresh horror strikes at the raw place, and makes it quiver worse than before.

I know you don't like my unhappy moods because they are so self-absorbed. But what am I to do? If you have any prescription I will consider it. But I know of none – and my feeling is that it is not fair to associate with people unless I keep my despair to myself. *Please* write to me – here – I shall tell Smith[3] my address – probably I shan't stay long in any one place.

Your
B.

The very next day, however, Russell was jolted, at least momentarily, out of this mood of despair by a bit of political excitement. After the Leeds conference the provisional committee had started work setting up workers' and soldiers' councils. Russell had persuaded the NCF, though only by the narrowest margin, to seek representation on the councils. As a result on

---

1 This was probably the manuscript 'Why do men persist in living?' found among Morrell's papers. See *Papers*, vol. xiv, pp. 26–7.
2 The provisional government had not negotiated an end to Russia's participation in the war and, early in July, had started a new offensive which had now turned into a rout. Faced with mutinies, desertions, and unrest during the so-called 'July days', the government, now under the leadership of Aleksandr Kerensky, had lurched to the right and was using troops still loyal to it to put down dissent.
3 Frank Russell's butler. Russell was about to go on a holiday with Colette.

28 July Russell attended a meeting at the Brotherhood Church on Southgate Road to organize the London council. The government, which had welcomed the Kerensky revolution in March and been only mildly hostile to the Leeds conference, was now beginning to worry, and sterner measures were taken to prevent the formation of the councils. Leaflets were posted in pubs around the church denouncing the group as German spies and a large drunken mob broke into the building and attacked those inside. Several people were hurt and Russell would have been among them but for the intervention of the unknown woman mentioned in the next letter. The belated arrival of the police to save him was the result of circumstances that Russell learnt of only afterwards and gave him one of his best stories of the war:

> Two of the drunken viragos began to attack me with their boards full of nails. While I was wondering how one defended oneself against this type of attack, one of the ladies among us went up to the police and suggested that they should defend me. The police, however, merely shrugged their shoulders. 'But he is an eminent philosopher', said the lady, and the police still shrugged. 'But he is famous all over the world as a man of learning', she continued. The police remained unmoved. 'But he is the brother of an earl', she finally cried. At this, the police rushed to my assistance.
>
> (*Autobiography*, vol. ii, p. 32)

Though Russell goes on to say he went home in a mood of 'deep dejection', this was not how he described it to Ottoline later the same day.

[To Ottoline Morrell] **[London]**
28 July 1917

I got shaken out of the mood of doubt and depression I was in by the events at our meeting this afternoon which was broken up. A vast crowd of roughs and criminals (paid) led, or rather guided from behind, by a few merely foolish soldiers (Colonials) broke in – it was only due to great self-restraint on the part of the delegates that there was no bloodshed. It was really very horrible. There were two utterly bestial women with knotted clubs, who set to work to thwack all the women of our lot that they could get at. The roughs had horrible degraded faces. The crowd outside as we were leaving was very fierce – several women had almost all their clothes torn off their backs. But absolutely no one showed the faintest trace of fear. Most women would have been terrified, but ours were not even flustered.

I realized vividly how ghastly the spirit of violence is, and how utterly I repudiate it, on whatever side it may be. The mob is a terrible thing when it wants blood. The young soldiers were pathetic, thinking we were their enemies. They all believed we were in the pay of the Kaiser.

At one moment they all made a rush at me, and I was in considerable danger – but a woman (I don't know who) hurled herself between me and them. They hesitated to attack her – and then the police appeared. She showed wonderful courage.

I found the whole thing bracing. I realized that there are things that I believe in and that it is worth living for – love, gentleness, and understanding.

The mob got in by smashing the doors, before our proceedings had begun. It is strange how the world loves its enemies rather than its friends.

Goodbye. Thank you for your letter this morning. Every word of it is true.[1] I shall come back to real things in time – meanwhile one must exist somehow.

Your
    B.

---

1 Ottoline's long (and largely illegible) reply to the previous letter.

Source: Logicomix (Bloomsbury 2009)

Up The Backside!

How is it Nottingham now has Parliament Street (Upper and Lower), when people once strode along The Backside?

'... One Rouse, an inhabitant, a man of some property, but a little deranged in his mind, offered himself as a candidate at an election to serve in Parliament, some few years since, in one of his mad fits. He treated his companions, the lower orders of the electors, with ale, purl, and sometimes rhubarb, which he strongly recommended to all as an excellent thing for the constitution. He not liking the name of the place he lived in, The Backside, and always thinking of the dignity he coveted, was at the expense of placing boards at some of the conspicuous corners of the passages, on which was written Parliament Street, whence he was to pass to his seat in Westminster Hall. Some of these boards are still remaining; the man is sunk into the grave, but the street has effectually got a name, perhaps for ages.'

Thoroton's History of Nottinghamshire: volume 2
Republished with large additions by John Throsby (1790)

"Admire the rich Abodes of the opulent, the Grove, the Lawns and Flora's beauties; But seek the religious Ruin, the Grave and the Tomb, for calm contemplation."

J. Wigley del. et sculp.

Africa Genocide

John Daniels

John Daniels established the Russell Press. He discusses Michael Deibert's The Democratic Republic of Congo: Between Hope and Despair *and* Robin Philpot's Rwanda and the Scramble for Africa.

Two books on Central Africa, specifically the two nations of the Democratic Republic of Congo and the Republic of Rwanda, complement each other, as the reader will soon discover. It will become clear why Rwanda, such a relatively small country (at least by African standards), has had such a profound effect on the vastness that is the Congo. Paramount in this context we should remember the enormous resources that are to be found in the Congo and how important they are to the modern Western way of life, not forgetting the relatively recent Chinese interest. The list of mineral resources illustrates the Congo's riches: gold, diamonds, cobalt, coltan, copper, cassiterite and, of course, timber from the extensive rainforest. These assets alone are enough to provoke the interest of the economically powerful. Could it be that this very 'interest' might be the primary reason for the Congo's travails with its poverty, killings, famines and endemic diseases, many of which are easily cured; that these very resources are a curse rather than a blessing?

Reviewing another book on the Congo, *Dancing in the Glory of Monsters*, *The Economist* magazine states 'Five million people have died in the Congo in a war that no one understands'. After reading Michael Deibert's book you will understand a lot more about the political history of the Congo, particularly over the last 20 years. The first European contact was with Dutch and Portuguese traders in what was then the Kingdom of Kongo. Although its geographical extent did not exactly correspond to the present day republic stretching over what are now adjacent countries, the interlopers would have found a relatively advanced society. As one would expect, this kingdom, given a great river and an outlet to the sea, was a centre for trade and therefore politically and economically powerful. The horrific and cruel slave trade was an important source of wealth creation for the kingdom's rulers and their Western overlords. Intensive resource exploitation, however, started with the period of Belgian rule. As a personal fiefdom of Leopold II, the Congo became a byword for the worst kind of imperialist exploitation with forced labour, killings, famines, mutilation and torture.

The Democratic Republic of Congo opens the modern period in 1960 with the declaration of the Congo's independence from Belgium, and the bestial treatment and eventual death of the man who could possibly have stopped the Congo's descent into a manmade hell – Patrice Lumumba. He headed the largest party, the *Mouvement National Congolias* (MNC), and was made Prime Minister of a coalition government. Lumumba, it became clear, was to be no neo-colonial lackey and committed the ultimate sin for those Cold War times: he asked for Soviet military and economic assistance. Of course, such a move was calculated to bring down the ire of not only Belgium and its European allies (Britain included), but also, crucially, the United States. With internal tensions rising, a shaky coalition government, and the secessionist activities of Moise Tshombe and the Belgian mining company, Union Minière, in Katanga, the outlook after independence seemed very difficult. These factors, together with a Congolese army of questionable loyalties, being under almost complete command of Belgian officers, had Lumumba with his back to the wall. Neither were UN peacekeepers any help; quite the contrary, in fact. They had been drafted in by the Security Council, arriving, ominously, in US transport aircraft on the 15th July 1960. The first Congolese President was Joseph Kasa-Vubu, and his party was in a distinctly uneasy government coalition with the MNC. In September 1960, Kasa-Vubu dismissed Lumumba and, later that year, placed him under house arrest. Lumumba escaped, but was recaptured and handed back to government troops who received the direct order, probably from Mobutu, then head of the army, and Kasa-Vubu to dispatch him to the tender mercies of Moise Tshombe in Katanga. Undoubtedly, all the plotters, both national and international, have blood on their hands, being aware that they were sending Lumumba to his certain death. From the inception of their capture, Lumumba and two party colleagues captured with him, were mercilessly beaten and tortured with little or no attempt to disguise the fact. The horrendous tale of Lumumba's last days can be read in *The Assassination of Lumumba* by

Ludo De Witte (Verso, 2001). This makes clear that his death was connived at or tacitly agreed by the Belgian Government, President Eisenhower, JFK, Allen Dulles (head of the CIA), Harold Macmillan, King Baudouin, and probably elements in the UN.

After Lumumba's death, Mobuto, Chief of Staff of the Congolese Army, became the real power in the land, with Kasa-Vubu still President, and with Tshombe as Prime Minister for a time. Kasa-Vubu's charade staggered on for some three years but, as Deibert states, he was left 'presiding over a series of weak governments, with Mobuto largely pulling the strings behind the scenes'. An uprising by Lumumba's supporters, known as the Simba Rebellion, overran nearly half the country, but was crushed by a combination of the National Congolese Army led by mercenaries, UN and Belgian troops, and US air-power. Two participants in the rebellion were Laurent Kabila (of whom more later) and the Cuban revolutionary, Che Guevara. Kasa-Vubu dismissed Tshombe and Mobutu, sensing the time was propitious, and seized direct executive power. Thus began the reign of Mobutu Sese Seko Kuku Ngbendu wa Za Banga who, renaming the nation Zaire, was to rule for 32 years. The book goes into some detail about Mobutu's rule, painting a picture of a repressive dictatorship, with contempt for human rights and the wellbeing of its people. Killings, poverty and torture typified his regime, whilst he always kept on the right side of the Western powers through a combination of tolerance towards foreign economic exploitation and virulent anti-communism. There is one feature of Mobutu's rule that by its degree was exceptional: corruption. Such was its extent that, towards the end of his regime, the state infrastructure hardly functioned at all. The system was not just corrupt; corruption *was* the system. Mutinies amongst ordinary soldiers, often over pay, were frequent, leading to riots, looting and killing. At the same time, some officers, perhaps showing misdirected entrepreneurial zeal, were privately selling off their equipment and weaponry. Politically, however, by the 1990s, the world had changed and it was no longer enough to be a bastion of anti-communism to win favour with the West.

Having set the scene in the earlier chapters, the text now becomes enveloped in the labyrinthine world of Congo's political, military and ethnic factionalism which, together with the regional and international factors, has helped to manufacture and intensify its descent into a cauldron of unspeakable horrors. Deibert carefully relates the intricacies of the history of this period which, in their complexity, make it impossible to summarise here. We can only pick out the major players and events. The key event is the invasion of the Eastern Congo by Rwandan forces, and its bringing together of the different anti-Mobutu forces under the leadership of Laurent Kabila. This bringing together of the disparate opposition in the *Alliance des Forces Démocratiques pour la Libération du Congo-Zaïre* (AFDL) signified a period of intensive warfare.

The invasion by Rwandan forces was ostensibly to halt incursions into Rwanda by Hutu *interahamwe* and to stop the latter's control of Hutu refugee camps in Zaire. Mobutu, terminally ill and without either popular support or a loyal and well-armed fighting force at his disposal, fled and, in 1997, Kabila was installed as President of a newly named Democratic Republic of Congo. Mobutu, having served the interests of the West loyally for so long, must have become more and more of an embarrassment with his outlandish peccadilloes so the US was happy for their trusted lieutenants, Kagame and Museveni, to unseat him, even if it meant the deaths of millions. Later in 1998, Kabila demanded the withdrawal of all foreign forces, his former allies, from Congolese territory. Rwandan and Ugandan forces advanced on the capital, Kinshasa, but were repulsed by a combined military force consisting of troops from Angola, Zimbabwe and Namibia. Subsequently, peace treaties and declarations were made against a background of continuing conflict, with Ugandan and Rwandan proclamations of withdrawal accompanied by accusations that they had left surrogate anti-Kinshasa movements to continue the conflict.

On top of all this were ethnic conflicts, particularly the Hutu-Tutsi killings, which now spilled over from Rwanda into the Congo, fanned by factional differences and the problem of Tutsis that had lived for several generations in the Eastern Congo, the so-called *Banyamulenge* people. Other elements that make up this tangle of interests are the local defence forces, the Mai-Mai, who probably had no permanent relationships with other groups and movements but functioned on a purely local basis. Local warlords and politicians often associated with them, or possessing their own armed supporters, made for further factional violence. The political-military situation might be confusing, but there is clarity about the horror that was inflicted on the people of the Congo. All parties were capable of carrying out unbelievable levels of killing, sexual violence and general destruction of infrastructure. A UN observer comments on the massacres carried out by the *Rwanda Patriotic Army* and the AFDL on Hutu refugees:

> '... the apparent systematic nature of the massacres ... suggests that the numerous deaths cannot be attributed to the hazards of war or seen as collateral damage. The majority of the victims were children, women and elderly people and the sick, who were often undernourished and posed no threat to the attacking force.' (page 60)

In January 2001, Laurent Kabila was assassinated by one of his bodyguards and, after a shaky start, his son Joseph took over as President. Four of the main opposition groups were co-opted into drawing up a new constitution and, in 2006, elections confirmed Joseph Kabila as President. All this time the conflict and mayhem continued in the East of the country. All the twists and turns of the history of these events are carefully catalogued by Deibert, but it is easy to get lost in this thicket of information. This again is not helped by the impossibility of remembering a total of 108 organisational groupings, there being three-and-a-half pages of acronyms! As to the reason for all these conflicts, and particularly the level of violence towards civilians, the author manages to avoid the usual stereotypical reasons used to explain it, such as the barbarism of the 'dark continent'. Not that he underplays the violence, using in the moving prologue the testimony of a farmer who had to endure the loss of most of his family and village to the actions of a group of marauding soldiers. *The Democratic Republic of Congo: Between Hope and Despair* has relatively little to say about the responsibility of the great powers for the turmoil in Central Africa after the fall of Mobutu, but it does mention debt and the imposition of structural adjustment strategies imposed on the Congo. Criticism is also made of the inept UN forces in the Congo, who were incapable of keeping the warring factions apart with the inadequate manpower at their disposal, despite being the largest peace-keeping force under the UN's control.

Not only was this recent period in the Congo's history one of violent turmoil and struggle for power, but also, as the author states, one of 'armed robbery of epic proportions'. This 'robbery' was committed by neighbouring countries, Congolese officials and, of course, the international business community. This country 'containing 1,100 different mineral substances' should have been, according to the author, 'an economic and political powerhouse' which 'should stride across the continent'. Alas, this is far from the case and violence still rumbles on in the East with clashes between the Mai-Mai militias, M23, the Lord's Resistance Army, and other armed groups with government forces.

* * *

Rwanda, such a small country in comparison with its neighbour, has had and continues to have an enormous influence on the Democratic Republic of Congo. Robin Philpot's book, *Rwanda and the Scramble for Africa: From Tragedy to Useful Imperial Fiction,* is a far more polemical tract and the author has little hesitation in contradicting what he calls the

'Information Dominance' of the mainly Western media when it comes to the facts about the 'Rwanda Genocide'. Briefly, most journalistic and political opinion favours the idea that the killings in Rwanda were planned by elements in the Hutu government and were genocidal in nature. The word genocide, often used to describe the events of 1994 in Rwanda, may have lost some of its resonance through over-use, but that upwards of 500,000 Rwandans lost their lives is indisputable. Philpot is concerned that these events have not been truthfully reported: that we have been misled as to where responsibility lies for both the context and the reasons that ignited the orgy of killings. Firstly, he seeks to deny that the *Rwandan Patriotic Front* (RPF) and its charismatic leader, Paul Kagame, represented a force that halted the killings; in fact, the killing continues but has transferred to the Eastern Congo. Kagame received his initial military training with the Ugandan rebel forces led by Yoweri Museveni against Milton Obote's dictatorial regime. He rose to be Museveni's head of intelligence and later received further military education at the US Army Command and General Staff College in Fort Leavenworth. He was later to become Vice-President, is now the President of Rwanda, and stands accused of acting ruthlessly against former political allies and oppositionists.

Although acute violence between the two ethnic groups had begun in the 1960s, the present cycle of violence commenced in 1990 when Tutsis living in Uganda formed the *Rwandan Patriotic Army* (RPA), according to Philpot really an adjunct to the Ugandan army. They were equipped with the latest modern weapons and therefore had little difficulty in invading and occupying the northern part of Rwanda, causing about 800,000 Hutu small farmers to move south, thus becoming internal refugees. In 1993, the government of Rwanda's President Habyarimana was forced by events and Western pressure to agree to a ceasefire and a power-sharing agreement with the RPA invaders. The Habyarimana Government has been accused of being systematically corrupt (Andy Storey, 'Structural Adjustment, State Power & Genocide: the World Bank & Rwanda', *Review of African Political Economy No. 89, 2001*), but Rwanda during his period of office had to endure the benefice of the World Bank and a structural adjustment package. In 1994, the plane carrying the Hutu presidents of Rwanda and Burundi was shot down, killing both of them and the crew. Philpot makes the case that the ceasefire allowed the Rwandan Patriotic Army to infiltrate support cells into the villages and towns and that, after the plane was shot down, they participated in the mass violence that took place. It was therefore not a simple case of Hutus killing Tutsis. The author and an increasing number of commentators also think that whoever was responsible for the assassination and the downing of the plane must have realised that this would lead to a bloodbath. Additionally, it would also have given the Rwandan Patriotic Army an excuse to break the ceasefire and advance on Kigali, ostensibly to halt the mayhem.

The Hutu killers, the *interahamwe,* were forced to flee across the border to Zaire, along with probably 2 million mostly innocent Hutus, who were fearful that they might be accused of complicity in the killings. The new government in Rwanda claimed that in order to capture and put on trial the *interahamwe,* and to prevent hit-and-run cross-border incursions, it was necessary that the Rwandan Patriotic Army should invade that area of the Congo where the Rwandan refugees were located. Of course, publicly, Kagame and the RPA asked the refugees to return if they were innocent but few actually did so, opting to stay in the Congo even if it meant terrible suffering at the hands of the armed groups. In the supposed hunt for the *interahamwe,* as Deibert also makes clear in his book, the atrocities endured by those inhabiting the Eastern Congo were almost beyond belief. Distasteful as it is, the balance sheet of killing (probably over 5 million) shows a much higher number for Rwandans and others being killed in the Congo in comparison with the Rwandan 'genocide'. Many of the attacks on the Hutu camps in Zaire are documented in the Deibert book.

Tutsis represented some 15 per cent of the Rwandan population, but they had always occupied a leading position in colonial society (after the colonisers themselves). They were selected by both the Belgian and German colonists for administrative, business and other leading roles in the colonies of Rwanda and Burundi. Philpot suggests that, because they were a minority, the Tutsis could never realise their goal through electoral mechanisms and, as a result, opted to gain what they could by force. Philpot sees the 1990 military encroachment by the Rwandan Patriotic Army from Uganda, aided by Yoweri Museveni, as invasion by another country (the primary war crime as defined by the Nuremberg hearings) and a direct attack on the democratic rights of the Hutu majority. Not only had they granted power-sharing during the meeting at Arusha in Tanzania, but they also agreed to a UN mission to monitor the agreement. As far as the Habyarimana government was concerned, the civil war was over – and then came the assassinations!

Boutros Boutros-Gali has spoken out publicly about the Rwanda killings, stating that 'the Rwanda genocide was 100 per cent American responsibility', so it is no surprise that the US fought tooth and nail to have the UN Secretary General restricted to only one term of office when two was the norm. This is what Philpot's book aims to expose: the covert activities of the US to cement a controlling interest in Central Africa, which means harnessing its vast material resources, thus placing the US in a competitive situation *vis-à-vis* the dominant colonial power, France. American influence and pressure from the International Monetary Fund had already caused the abandonment of a more enlightened programme of social action in place of the usual structural adjustment provisions. The book tackles head-on the assertions of the mainstream narrative, which has been so successfully cultivated by Paul Kagame, whose presentational skills must have received top marks when he was on his military course at Fort Leavenworth. It was Kagame who led the Rwandan Patriotic Front in its invasion of Northern Rwanda, causing some 800,000 Hutu small-scale farmers to become internal refugees in their own country. In this context the legitimate government was pressurised by Western governments to accept power-sharing with the RPF forces, which was a largely Ugandan equipped and drafted force. For Philpot, the fate of the Rwandan Government was sealed at the Arusha Peace Accords in 1993 as they were forced to carry out polices which undermined their own power base.

Philpot takes to task some of the many non-governmental organisations that had begun to proliferate in Rwanda after Arusha, as many were supportive of the mainstream view, siding with the Rwandan Patriotic Front. A number of these NGOs set up a commission to investigate the human rights abuses by the Rwandan Government of Habyarimana. Philpot has made a number of telling criticisms of the methodology of the Commission, but the most glaring omission was its failure to say anything at all about the charge of aggression, which could be levelled at those who invaded another country and thus started the conflict. As the author points out, this was the primary charge faced by the Nazi leaders at the Nuremburg trials: that they started a war of aggression. Particularly vociferous on behalf of supporting the Commission and its findings were two propagandists (there were many others) with the ear of the media: Alison des Forges and Phillip Gourevitch, the former a consultant at the US State Department and the latter the brother-in-law of Jamie Rubin, Madeleine Albright's public relations advisor. This assortment of scribes has, Philpot asserts, managed to foist upon the public a questionable narrative which this book helps to unpick. The International Criminal Tribunal for Rwanda (ICTR) stated after detailed investigation that Kagame and the Rwandan Patriotic Front were responsible for some of the killings after the presidential plane was downed. This was the opinion of the principal investigator, Michael Hourigan. When the evidence was presented to the Tribunal, prosecutor Louise Arbour (her appointment vetted by Madeleine Albright) closed down the investigation. The other service this book does is to resist the temptation to belittle Africa and African experience with nostrums of the colonial past. It focuses in particular on the conduct of the Tribunal and the fact that it has yet to find evidence of the Habyarimana Government plotting to organise 'genocide' against the Tutsi minority.

Robin Philpot is a Canadian, as was the head of the ineffective UN mission (ineffective in the sense that it did little to halt the killings), the force commander Romeo Dallaire, who aligned himself firmly with US machinations and whose hostility to the French was palpable. He refused offers of help from competent French investigators available nearby to examine the wreckage of the plane that was shot down, killing the Presidents of Rwanda and Burundi. He did this knowing that French nationals were also passengers on the plane, saying he had already spoken to the Americans and an investigative team was to be sent from Germany. The Western media soon began to speak of a 'plane crash' and, although the matter was raised in the UN Security Council and a thorough investigation demanded, we are still waiting for the truth of who was responsible. This was undoubtedly the trigger for the killings, as the perpetrators must have been aware. Paul Kagame has been held personally responsible by two 'former colleagues', according to the text. Kagame has vigorously denied he was responsible, so much so that in 2002 he brought a court case against his accuser, but the case seems to have been left in abeyance. Philpot makes a strong assertion that without the assassinations there would be a lot more people alive today, and even more if there had been a timely and massive enlargement of UN peace-keeping troops. In fact, the Americans made every effort to force the UN to withdraw what meagre troops were actually in position. The only reason for this could have been the need to allow the Rwandan Patriotic Front to get on with a swift advance on Kigali, the Rwandan capital. With its modern equipment generously supplied by its Western backers, the RPF was certainly capable of doing that and swept aside any Rwandan government troops in their path. With the advance of the RPF on the Rwandan capital, thousands fled into Zaire, away from the approaching army of vengeance, but, as Philpot and Deibert both make clear, the Congo was to be no safe haven, but a charnel house. Estimates of those killed in the Congo dwarf numerically those murdered in the massacres in Rwanda – a terrible vengeance was exacted on the vast numbers of innocents who had taken refuge there.

Justice should be seen to be done, and the undistorted truth should be available to all. However, De Witte's book about Lumumba's murder makes it clear that, until state documents are opened, particularly those of the Western powers that were involved, we will have only a partial picture.

Deibert and Philpot's books briefly mention commercial interests, but it would have been useful to have more detail on these, both indigenous and foreign capital. This is of particular importance when looking at the Congo. Of course, we are all aware of the evocative term 'blood diamonds', trade in which was extensive in Eastern Congo. Even Hollywood got in on the act with a major feature film called, aptly enough, 'Blood Diamond'. Now there is a new scramble for Africa, as the subtitle of the Rwanda book, *From Tragedy to Useful Imperial Fiction,* asserts. For example, the G8's *New Alliance for Food Security and Nutrition,* with its encouragement of the multinationals to invest in African agriculture, provides a guise for corporate expansion into the food markets of Africa at the expense of small-scale indigenous farmers. This will be dressed up with the usual verbiage, but the benefits to Africa will be few.

No doubt, these two books will be criticised by many media commentators, both from left and right. Judging by the treatment dished out to an earlier dissident publication which discussed the Rwanda 'Genocide' (*The Politics of Genocide* by Herman and Peterson, published by Monthly Review Press in 2010), it will not be long in coming. *The Politics of Genocide* was strongly attacked by George Monbiot, who is usually eminently sensible. Deibert and Philpot's books are an important contribution to the debate about what happened and is happening in Central Africa. They are polemical, but they are also compassionate and well aware of the tragedy which has enveloped this area of Africa. In spite of a blanket of media obfuscation, slowly but surely the message is beginning to get through that this is no simple tribal conflict and that there is something wrong with the dominant narrative. Western interests have moulded much of the context within which the drama has taken place, and to the present day continue to have a negative effect on a continent that has suffered so much.

Michael Deibert, **The Democratic Republic of Congo: Between Hope and Despair***, Zed Books, 260 pages, ISBN 978178032 345 9 paperback ISBN 9781780323466 £12.99, hardback £60.00*

Robin Philpot, **Rwanda and the Scramble for Africa: From Tragedy to Useful Imperial Fiction***, Baraka Books of Montreal, 274 pages, paperback ISBN 9781926824949 $24.95*

Postscript

On 24 September 2014, a remarkable documentary, *This World – Rwanda the Untold Story*, was broadcast on BBC2, presented and produced by Jane Corbin. It reinforces most of the argument and information provided in the two titles under review, and adds to the weight of evidence that Paul Kagame was responsible for downing the aircraft with the Presidents of Rwanda and Burundi aboard, together with policies and actions that resulted in the deaths of millions. It also provided evidence obtained by two US academics, Stam and Davenport of the University of Michigan, that when it came to genocide, the Hutus suffered numerically far more than the Tutsis. Also interviewed were dissident former members of Kagame's inner circle including his former military Chief of Staff, General Faustin Kayumba Nyamwasa. The latter was present at meetings where the downing of the presidential plane and the invasion of the Congo were actively discussed and initiated. Today, Rwanda is a fiercely repressive state where dissidents are murdered or silenced at home and in exile, and where 'democratic' elections are fixed to make sure that Kagame and his stooges are elected. Meanwhile, Kagame is lauded by Western politicians and much of the media, as a great democrat and an example to all of Africa, who stopped the genocide of 1994. The myths built up around Kagame are worthy of comparison with Joseph Stalin's falsification of history and personality cult. The documentary has truly nauseating footage of Tony Blair praising Kagame to the rooftops. Blair and former UK Foreign Secretary, William Hague, together with Bill Clinton, all participated in a rally in Rwanda to commemorate their version of the 1994 genocide.

The story of Africa has been one of exploitation and pillage, which has intensified over the last few decades, and we need to understand what is happening and counter the present thrust of neo-liberal policies. These policies have led to the impoverishment and erosion of state infrastructures, exemplified by thousands of lives lost in the present Ebola outbreak.

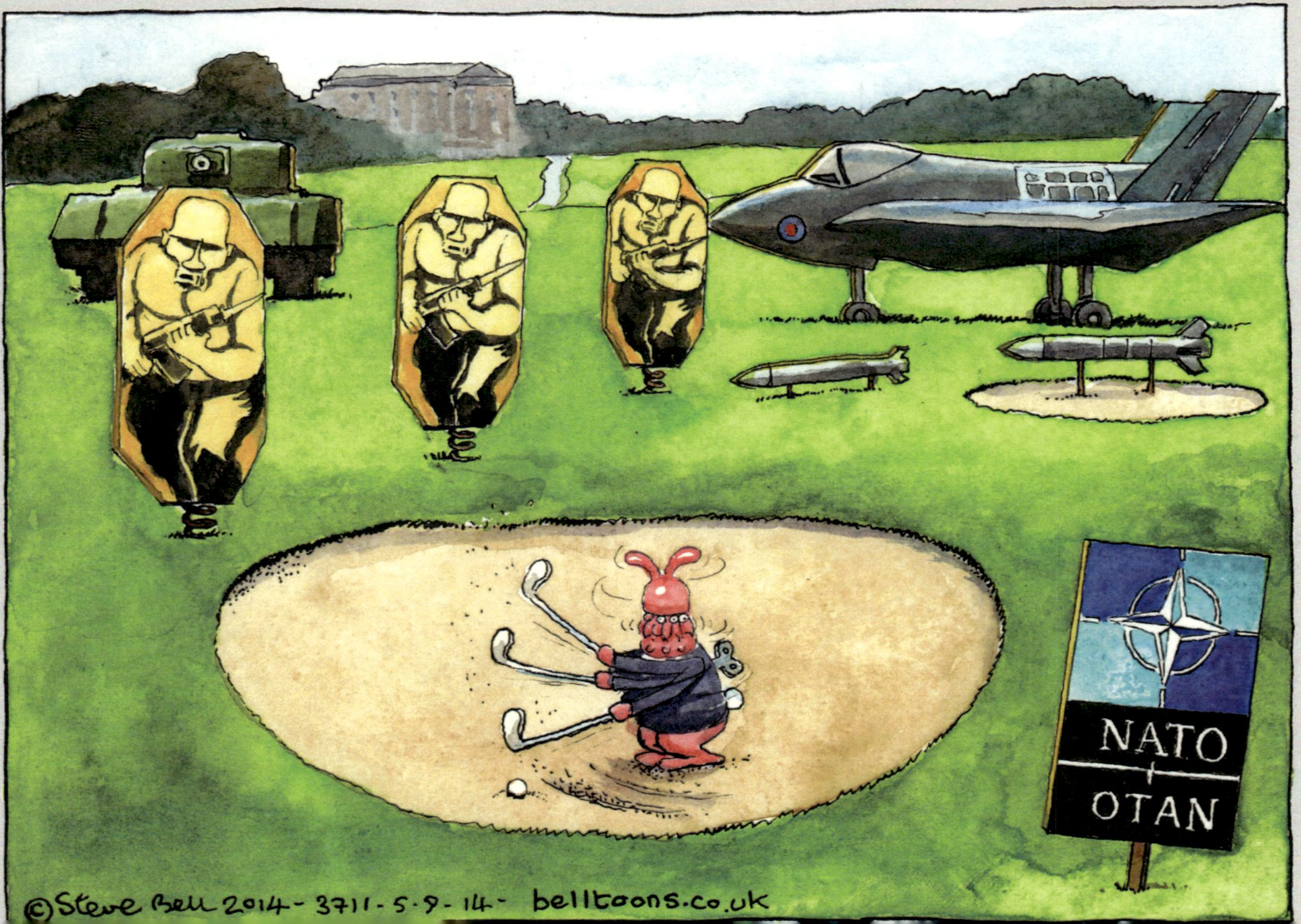
NATO
OTAN
©Steve Bell 2014- 3711- 5·9·14- belltoons.co.uk

NATO – NO, TA!

Tony Simpson

This Tony Simpson is editor of The Spokesman, *published in Nottingham. Others with the same name include the author of* No Bunkers Here, *a classic account of successful non-violent action in a Welsh community in the early 1980s, and a third Tony Simpson, based in Honiton, who writes letters to the* Morning Star.

'*Approaching along the M4 from the Severn Bridge, Newport is announced by a glowering Monte Cassino-like fortress above the wooded escarpment, which turns out to be a monstrous modern hotel. How on earth was this eyesore ever permitted? Well, such is the power of golf, the great hope for a diversified economic future. It was the HQ of the 2010 Ryder Cup.*'

Towns in Britain
Adrian Jones & Chris Matthews
(Five Leaves, 2014)

It was also the shakedown for heads of government and their retinues attending NATO's summit meeting in early September 2014. Incongruously, 'replicas' of armoured personnel carriers and the latest strike aircraft were parked around Celtic Manor's golf links while the world's press did its 30 seconds to camera. Was this an attempt to disabuse sceptical viewers that all the political and military brass might engage in some 19th hole junket?

What follows is based on the Russell Foundation's public statement at the time of the NATO Summit in Newport.

* * *

The leaders of 28 NATO member countries and many others gathered for a summit meeting in Newport, the third city of Wales, on 4/5 September 2014. For days together, this small city was besieged while fences, gates and barricades were erected to protect those attending. The cost was substantial, and there was considerable inconvenience to the people of Newport and to the thousands of peace movement activists who gathered there to protest at the nuclear-armed Alliance's profligacy and increasing belligerence. NATO's uselessness is never more apparent than when it rudely disrupts people's lives in order to exult in 65 costly years of existence.

It was with some foresight, in 1949, that the distinguished Irish Foreign Minister, Seán MacBride, rejected an invitation, sent through the American Ambassador in Dublin, to participate in a meeting to discuss the formation of the North Atlantic Alliance. Later, MacBride gave several reasons for his opposition:

> 'First of all I regarded NATO as being a rather dangerous military alliance that might well involve Europe in another war at more or less the wish of the United States. I could quite well see the American anti-communist view pushing NATO into a cold war first, and then into an active war.'

How prescient MacBride was. Nowadays, Russia may no longer be communist, but it remains the target of large-scale NATO expansion; in the Baltics, in Poland and elsewhere in central Europe, in the Balkans (Serbia included), around the Black Sea, especially in Georgia and Ukraine. Ukraine shares a long border with Russia. Planned missile 'defence' installations in Poland and Romania underline the aggressive posture towards Russia which the US maintains.

It should never be forgotten that the United States runs NATO in its own interests. When the US wanted to go to war in Afghanistan in 2001, immediately after 9/11, it spurned NATO's offers of assistance, made by the then Secretary-General, George Robertson. Only later did the US identify a useful, and expensive, role for NATO in that theatre of operations.

Be that as it may, Ireland had a particularly compelling reason not to join NATO, according to Mr MacBride:

> '... it was completely illogical for us to enter into a military alliance with Britain while a part of our country was still being occupied by British forces. We would be condoning and accepting the British occupation of Northern Ireland by entering a military alliance with Britain.'

The fundamentals of that situation endure, notwithstanding the real achievements of the peace process in Ireland. MacBride went on:

> 'I can't think of any good reason why Ireland should join NATO, then or now. NATO is a dangerous military alliance and I have noticed that there is a great deal of hesitancy among many of the NATO countries. I am very glad that we didn't join and that we didn't spend vast sums of money on quite unnecessary armament.'

There have been few statesmen with such clear vision. Currently, Ireland spends less than half of one per cent of its gross domestic product on the military, while Greece, which, like Ireland, has suffered greatly from austerity policies imposed by others, still spends more than NATO's two per cent target.

Seán MacBride developed his critique of NATO when accepting the Nobel Peace Prize in December 1974. He said:

> ' ... It would be foolish to underrate the massive influence of the organized lobbies of military-industrial complexes in the United States and Western Europe. They constitute an unseen and unmentioned powerful force operating silently in the corridors of NATO and of most Western governments. Their resources are unlimited and their influence is great. This constitutes a huge vested interest which works silently against General and Complete Disarmament.'

The world much needs statesmen with MacBride's experience and vision. Unfortunately, there was little sign of such in the ghastly halls of Celtic Manor, fenced off from the people of South Wales. Symbolically, that second-hand fence has now been offered to France to keep at bay the refugees of NATO'S wars in Libya and elsewhere, who gather at Calais *en route* to Britain.

NATO's profligacy has not gone unnoticed in The Netherlands, where the Court of Auditors are investigating. We publish their initial letter as The Netherlands prepares to host the NATO Parliamentary Assembly in November 2014, together with David Vine's perceptive analysis of contractors' profiteering amidst the US military's vast overseas estate, including the 'British Indian Ocean Territory' of Diego Garcia, where wars begin.

NATO's 'modest steps'

Saskia J. Stuiveling
Ellen M.A. van Schoten

The authors of the letter are, respectively, President and Secretary of the Netherlands Court of Auditors.

Anouchka van Miltenburg became President of the House of Representatives of The Netherlands in 2012. In October 2013, the Court of Auditors sent her this letter about problems with auditing NATO expenditure. In November 2014, the States General of The Netherlands will host the NATO Parliamentary Assembly, comprising 257 parliamentarians from 28 NATO member states, where this is sure to be a hot topic.

* * *

Date: 1 October 2013
Subject: Audit of NATO expenditure

Madam President,

In recent years we have informed the House of Representatives every year of our observations on the audit of NATO expenditure.[1] We observed that NATO was taking its first tentative steps towards more transparent accounts of its expenditure. We would like to assist NATO in this by analysing its funds flows. This letter first considers the current view provided of NATO's financial management and then presents our proposal to map out its funds flows.

Annual meeting of NATO member SAIs

The supreme audit institutions (SAIs) of the NATO member states met to discuss the annual report of *the International Board of Auditors for NATO (IBAN)* on 14 May 2013. IBAN audits all NATO's expenditure, which totalled more than €11 billion in 2012.[2]

Financial management remains a matter of concern
As in previous years the SAIs expressed their concern about the high number of qualified opinions. It is not clear precisely what happened with nearly a third of the funds; of the 44 opinions on the accuracy of the annual accounts, 13 were qualified and one was adverse. IBAN expressed its concerns about this outcome in its annual 2/3 report and acknowledged the need to make improvements. The SAIs agree with IBAN and look upon the proposed improvements as an important factor in the reforms NATO is currently implementing.

Modest steps towards greater accountability
We think NATO should keep and present transparent accounts of its use of the member states' contributions. NATO recently appointed a *Head of Financial Reporting* to report to NATO committees on financial matters. We remain in favour, however, of appointing a *Chief Financial Officer* (CFO) to the North Atlantic Council. A CFO would be better placed to put affairs in order because the position would have more power and would be in direct contact with the North Atlantic Council.

Last year NATO decided to take a modest step towards making its accounts public. With effect from 2013, NATO will publish its audit reports as a matter of principle unless they include sensitive information. To date, however, no audit reports have been published in accordance with this policy. Nor does NATO publish the annual financial statements underlying its audit reports. In our opinion, insisting on this should be given highest priority.

NATO world map

NATO has made some progress improving its financial management and transparency but still has a lot of work to do. We are now taking the initiative to explain NATO's funds flows – its income and expenses – so that taxpayers can see where the money is spent and gain an insight into *value for money* at NATO.

We will reconstruct and present NATO's funds flows on an interactive world map. The data underlying the map will be derived from public sources; from the outset, we will adhere to the principle of *open spending*. In the longer term, we will seek to present a world map of funds flows using *open data* provided by the NATO organisations and the member states. We can then present an up-to-date overview of the alliance's public funding and performance.

Financial and organisational transparency is part of an important social trend that governments and international organisations such as NATO cannot ignore if they wish to retain public support. More and more importance is being attached both nationally and internationally to user-friendly, interactive information on what public money is being spent on and what results are being achieved with it.[3] A good example of this trend is www.recovery.gov. Such initiatives complement the *Open Government Initiative*, which 20 of the 28 NATO member states have joined.[4] These initiatives also agree with the principles of good public administration as defined by the United Nations and others.[5]

We are working on the initiative in close consultation with the Ministries of Defence and of Foreign Affairs. The world map will be a working document that we will discuss with the relevant parties at NATO, the other NATO member states and fellow supreme audit institutions.

In conclusion

We expect to publish a first version of the world map to coincide with the Parliamentary Assembly in The Hague in 2014. We will continue to follow developments in NATO expenditure and the Parliamentary Assembly. Your critical stance in the Assembly will remain of utmost importance to improve NATO's financial management.

We will send a copy of this letter to the President of the Senate and to the Ministers of Defence and of Foreign Affairs.

Netherlands Court of Audit

Saskia J. Stuiveling
President

Ellen M.A. van Schoten
Secretary

Notes

1 House of Representatives, 2007-2008, appendix to RU07000022; House of Representatives, 2009-2010, 28 676, no. 91; House of Representatives, 2010-2011, 28 676, no. 115; House of Representatives, 2011-2012, 28 676, no. 136; and House of Representatives, 2012-2013, 28 676, no. 164
2 *International Board of Auditors for NATO – Annual Activities Report 2012.*
3 See the foreword to our report, State of Central Government Accounts (House of Representatives, 2012-2013, 33 605, no. 2)
4 See http:///www.opengovpartnership.org
5 See, for example,
   http://www.unescap.org/pdd/prs/ProjectActivities/Ongoing/gg/governance.pdf

Ice Cream

How military contractors reap billions from US military bases overseas

David Vine

David Vine is associate professor of anthropology at American University in Washington DC. He is the author of the forthcoming Base Nation: How American Military Bases Abroad Are Damaging National Security and Hurting Us All *(Metropolitan Books, 2015), and* Island of Shame: The Secret History of the US Military Base on Diego Garcia *(Princeton University Press, 2009). We reprint his article with grateful acknowledgements to* Monthly Review, *where it first appeared (Vol.66 no.3).*

'You whore it out to a contractor,' Major Tim Elliott said bluntly. It was April 2012, and I was at a swank hotel in downtown London attending 'Forward Operating Bases 2012', a conference for contractors building, supplying, and maintaining military bases around the world. IPQC, the private company running the conference, promised the conference would 'bring together buyers and suppliers in one location' and 'be an excellent platform to initiate new business relationships' through 'face-to-face contact that overcrowded trade shows cannot deliver.'[1] Companies sending representatives included major contractors like General Dynamics and the food services company Supreme Group, which has won billions in Afghan war contracts, as well as smaller companies like QinetiQ, which produces acoustic sensors and other monitoring devices used on bases. 'We're profiteers,' one contractor representative said to the audience in passing, with only a touch of irony.

Other than the corporate representatives and a couple of journalists, a few officers from NATO member militaries were on hand to speak. Major Elliott of the Royal Scots Brigades had offered his stark assessment while explaining how to build a military base that allows a base commander to 'forget the base itself' – that is, the work of running the base – and instead maximise his effectiveness outside the base.[2]

Of course, Elliott said, in wartime you won't get contractors to run a base without 'a shitload of money'. At times, he said, this has meant vast amounts of 'time, effort, and resources' are going 'just to keep a base running'. In Afghanistan, Elliott said he saw situations so bad that on one base there were private security guards protecting privately contracted cooks who were cooking for the same private security guards ... who were protecting the privately contracted cooks ... who were cooking for the private security guards ... who were protecting the privately contracted cooks, and on it went.

By the end of 2014 in Afghanistan, the US military will have closed, deconstructed, or vacated most of what were once around 800 military installations, ranging from small checkpoints to larger combat outposts to city-sized bases.[3] Previously, the military vacated 505 bases it built or occupied in Iraq.[4]

Despite the closure of these 1,000-plus installations, the US military will still occupy around 800 military bases outside the fifty states and Washington DC.[5] In addition to more than 4,000 domestic bases, this collection of extraterritorial bases is undoubtedly the largest in world history.[6]

US bases overseas have become a major mechanism of US global power in the post-Second World War era. Alongside postwar economic and political tools like the International Monetary Fund, the World Bank, and the United Nations, the collection of extraterritorial bases – like colonies for the European empires before it – became a major mechanism for 'maintaining [US] political and economic hegemony,' advancing corporate economic and political interests, protecting trade routes, and allowing control and influence over territory vastly disproportionate to the land bases actually occupy.[7] Without a collection of colonies, the United States has used its bases, as well as periodic displays of military might, to keep wayward nations within the rules of an economic and political system favourable to itself.[8]

Building and maintaining this global base presence has cost US taxpayers billions of dollars. While the military once built and maintained its forts, bases, and naval stations, since the US war in Vietnam, private military contractors have increasingly constructed and run this global collection of bases, foreshadowing and helping to fuel broader government privatization efforts. During this unprecedented period, major corporations – US and foreign – have increasingly benefited from the taxpayer dollars that have gone to base contracting.

After an extensive examination of government spending data and contracts (as part of a larger five-year investigation of US bases abroad), my calculations show the Pentagon has dispersed around $385 billion in taxpayer-funded contracts to private companies for work outside the United States, mainly on bases, between the onset of the war in

Afghanistan in late 2001 and 2013 alone. The total is nearly double the entire State Department budget over the same period (and, of course, these overseas contracts represent only a portion of the total Pentagon budget, which totalled trillions over this period). While some of the contract moneys are for things like weapons procurement and training, rather than for bases and troop support, the thousands of contracts believed to be omitted from these tallies thanks to government accounting errors make the numbers a reasonable reflection of the everyday moneys flowing to private contractors to support the country's global base collection. Because of the secrecy surrounding military budgets as well as the Pentagon's poor accounting practices, the true total may be significantly higher.

Almost a third of the total – more than $115 billion – was concentrated among the top ten corporate recipients alone. Many of the names scoring the biggest profits are familiar: former Halliburton subsidiary Kellogg Brown & Root, private security company DynCorp, BP. Others are less well known: Agility, Fluor, Bahrain Petroleum Company. The complete list includes major transnational construction firms, large food service providers, the world's biggest oil companies, and thousands upon thousands of smaller companies receiving government contracts.

Others have also benefited – financially, politically, and professionally – from the huge collection of bases overseas. High-ranking officials in the military and the Pentagon bureaucracy, members of Congress (especially members of the armed services and appropriations committees), lobbyists, and local and national-level politicians in countries accommodating bases have all reaped rewards.

My investigation into base contracting abroad also reveals that base spending has been marked by spiralling expenditures, the growing use of uncompetitive contracts (and contracts lacking incentives to control costs), and outright fraud – in addition to the repeated awarding of non-competitive contracts to companies with histories of fraud and abuse. Financial irregularities have been so common that any attempt to document the misappropriation of taxpayer funds at bases globally would be a mammoth effort. In the Afghanistan and Iraq wars alone, the Commission on Wartime Contracting (which Congress established to investigate waste and abuse) has estimated that there has been $31–$60 billion in contracting fraud during the wars, with most of it involving bases in and around Afghanistan and Iraq.[9] In Singapore, at least four Navy officials have recently been charged with receiving bribes in the form of cash, gifts, and sexual services in exchange for providing a contractor with inside information and helping to inflate the company's billing. Globally, billions of dollars are likely wasted or misused every year.

Proponents of outsourcing the work of building, running, and supplying bases overseas argue that contractors save government and taxpayer money while allowing the military, as Major Elliott suggested, to focus on its combat duties. Research suggests that this is often not the case. Contractors tend to provide base (and other) services at higher costs than the military itself.[10] While contracting overseas has helped build and maintain a global network of bases that has supported the US government's geopolitical and geoeconomic aims – and US corporate interests – worldwide, foreign bases have become an important source of profit-making in their own right that have diverted hundreds of billions of taxpayer dollars from pressing domestic needs.

The Base World

Although some of the bases in the base world, like the naval station at Guantánamo Bay, Cuba, date to the late nineteenth century, most were built or occupied during the Second World War. (It is important to remember, however, that most of today's domestic bases, from the continental United States to Hawai'i and Alaska, occupy land that was once 'abroad'.) President Franklin D. Roosevelt acquired many of today's overseas bases in his 'destroyers for bases' deal with Britain. Acquisitions accelerated and continued through to the end of the war. By 1945, the United States occupied more than 30,000 installations at more than 2,000 base sites globally.[11]

While the number of US bases overseas fluctuated during the Cold War and declined by around 60 per cent after the Cold War's end, seventy years after the Second World War and more than sixty years after the Korean War, there are still 179 US base sites in Germany, 109 in Japan, and 83 in South Korea – among scores more dotting the planet in places like Aruba and Australia, Bahrain and Bulgaria, Colombia, Kenya, Qatar, and Yemen, just to name a few.[12] The bases range in size from small radar installations to massive air bases. While the Pentagon considers most of its overseas base sites 'small installations or locations', it defines 'small' as having a reported value of up to $800 million.[13] At the height of the wars in Iraq and Afghanistan, the total number of bases outside the fifty states and Washington DC probably numbered around 2,000. Today, the total remains around 800 (although the Pentagon does not even have an accurate count).

And the US military presence abroad is actually even larger. There are the Navy's eleven aircraft carriers – a kind of floating base, or as the Navy tellingly refers to them, 'four and a half acres of sovereign US territory'.[14]

There is also a significant, and growing, military presence in space, with space bases and weapons in development featuring names like 'Rods from God'.

Globally, the Pentagon occupies more than 28 million acres (97 per cent domestically), which is about the size the State of New York and bigger than all of North Korea. The military's buildings alone cover 2.2 billion square feet of space – almost three times that of Wal-Mart. McDonald's, too, pales in comparison with some 35,000 stores compared to the Pentagon's 291,000 buildings.[15] A more apt comparison is the total number of US embassies and consulates abroad. As a physical manifestation of the country's diplomatic tools, the 278 embassies and consulates worldwide represent about one-third the total number of bases and occupy far less territory. By my very conservative calculations, total expenditures to maintain bases and troops overseas probably reached $175 billion in fiscal year 2012.[16]

Peeling the potatoes and bringing home the bacon

Once upon a time, the military, not contractors, built and ran US bases. Soldiers, sailors, marines, airmen, and airwomen built the barracks, cleaned the clothes, and peeled the potatoes. This started changing during the Vietnam War, when Brown & Root began building major military installations in South Vietnam as part of a contractor consortium.[17] The company, which later became known as KBR, enjoyed deep ties with President Lyndon Johnson dating to the 1930s, leading to well-founded suspicions that Johnson steered contracts to Brown & Root.[18]

The use of contractors grew as the war in Vietnam continued. Amid nationwide resistance to the draft, contractors were one way to solve a labour problem that became permanent with the end of conscription in 1973. Militaries always need bodies to have a fighting force. In the era of the 'all-volunteer force', hiring contractors reduced the need to recruit new service members. In practice, the government passed the labour problem to contractors, who have generally searched the globe for the cheapest possible workers. Frequently, they have been Filipinos and other often formerly colonised non-US citizens willing to work for much less than uniformed troops. Additionally, the government and contractors often avoid paying for the health care, retirement, and other benefits provided to US troops.

A broader rise in the privatisation of formerly government services only accelerated the trend in the military. Without forced conscription, the military was also under pressure to retain troops once they joined. Keeping troops and their families happy with an increasingly diverse array of comforts played an important part in retaining the military's labour force. Especially at bases abroad, military leaders sought to mitigate the challenges of overseas tours with a generally cushier lifestyle than troops could afford at home. With time, troops, families, and, importantly, politicians came to expect elevated and ever-rising living standards not just at peacetimes bases, but in war zones as well. To deliver this lifestyle, the military would pay contractors with increasing generosity.

By the first Gulf War in 1991, one out of every hundred deployed personnel was a contractor. During military operations later in the 1990s in Somalia, Rwanda, Haiti, Saudi Arabia, Kuwait, and especially the Balkans, Brown & Root received more than $2 billion in base-support and logistics contracts for construction and maintenance, food services, waste removal, water production, transportation services, and much more.[19] In the Balkans alone, Brown & Root built 34 bases. The largest, Camp Bondsteel in Kosovo, covered 955 acres and included two gyms and other sports facilities, extensive dining and entertainment facilities, two movie theatres, coffee bars, and a post exchange ('PX') for shopping. Describing off-duty soldiers, a US Army representative told *USA Today*, 'We need to get these guys pumping iron and licking ice cream cones, whatever they want to do'. By contrast, military personnel from other NATO countries lived in existing apartments and factories.[20]

By the second Gulf War, contractors represented roughly half of all deployed personnel in Iraq. The company now known as KBR employed more than 50,000 people in the warzone. That is the equivalent of five divisions or one hundred army battalions.[21] City-sized bases became known for their Burger Kings, Starbucks, and car dealerships, their air conditioning, ice cream, and steak.[22] Although recent fiscal constraints have meant some increase in periodic kitchen ('KP') duty, for most in the military, the days of peeling potatoes are long gone.

Contracts, contracts, contracts

Figuring out who has been winning all the contracts for the increasingly comfortable military lifestyle was not easy. Between the secrecy surrounding military contracting and the profoundly unreliable nature of Pentagon accounting, it is difficult to determine who has been benefiting from the growth in base contracting. Because the government does not compile many aggregated lists of contract winners, I had to pick through hundreds of thousands of government contracts from publicly available data and research scores of companies worldwide. I used the same methodology for tracking funds as the Commission on Wartime Contracting, which Congress established to investigate waste and abuse in Afghanistan and Iraq.[23] This allowed me to compile a list of every Pentagon contract with a 'place of performance' – that is, the country where most of a contract's work is performed – outside the United States between the start of the Afghan war in October 2001 (fiscal year 2002) and May 2013.

There were 1.7 million contracts.

Scrolling through 1.7 million spreadsheet rows (more than can fit into a single Microsoft Excel file) offered a dizzying feel for the immensity of the Pentagon's activities and the money spent globally. Generally, the companies winning the largest contracts have been providing one (or more) of five things: Construction, Operations and Maintenance, Food, Fuel, and Security.

But among the 1.7 million contracts, the breadth was remarkable. There was one for $43 for sand in South Korea and another for a $1.7 million fitness centre in Honduras. There was the $23,000 for sports drinks in Kuwait, $53 million in base support services in Afghanistan, and everything from $73 in pens to $301 million for army industrial supplies in Iraq.

Cheek by jowl, I found the most basic services, the most banal purchases, and the most ominous acquisitions, including concrete sidewalks, a traffic light system, diesel fuel, insect fogger, shower heads, black toner, a 59" desk, unskilled labourers, chaplain supplies, linen for 'distinguished visitor' rooms, easy chairs, gym equipment, flamenco dancers, the rental of six sedans, phone cards, a 50" plasma screen, billiards cues, XBox 360 games and accessories, Slushie machine parts, a hot dog roller, scallops, shrimp, strawberries, asparagus, and toaster pastries, as well as hazardous waste services, a burn pit, ammo and clips, bomb disposal services, blackout goggles for detainees, and confinement buildings.

Not surprisingly, given the recent wars and the huge number of bases that have enabled and supported the wars and occupations, contractors have won the most taxpayer dollars in Afghanistan and Iraq. With more than 1,300 installations between the two countries, corporations received around $160 billion in contracts between 2001 and 2013. In Kuwait, where hundreds of thousands of troops deployed to Iraq, corporations enjoyed $37.2 billion in contracts. The next four countries where military contractors have received the largest contracts are those that have generally hosted the largest number of bases and the largest number of troops since the Second World War: Germany ($27.8 billion in contracts), South Korea ($18.2 billion), Japan ($15.2 billion), and Britain ($14.7 billion).

Top Ten Countries by Pentagon Spending, Funds Fiscal Year 2002-April 2013

Country	Total (billions)
1. Iraq	89.1
2. Afghanistan	69.8
3. Kuwait	37.2
4. Germany	27.8
5. South Korea	18.2
6. Japan	15.2
7. United Kingdom	14.7
8. United Arab Emirates	10.1
9. Bahrain	6.9
10. Italy	5.8

Source: http://usaspending.gov
Note: Canada and Saudi Arabia would have also made the ten, however, those contracts are for the most part unrelated to the limited US military presence in each country, and thus are excluded from this list.

The $385 billion total is at best a rough estimate because Pentagon and government accounting practices are so poor; the federal data system has even been called 'dysfunctional'.[24] The real totals are almost surely higher, especially considering the secretive nature of Pentagon budgets. Black budgets and CIA contracts for paramilitary activities alone could add tens of billions of dollars in overseas base spending.[25]

The unreliable and opaque nature of the data becomes clear given that the top recipient of Pentagon contracts abroad is not a company at all, but 'miscellaneous foreign contractors'.[26] That is, almost 250,000 contracts totalling nearly $50 billion, or 12 per cent of the total, have gone to recipients that the Pentagon has not identified publicly. As the Commission on Wartime Contracting explains, 'miscellaneous foreign contractors' is a catch-all 'often used for the purpose of obscuring the identification of the actual contractor[s]'.[27]

The reliability of the data worsens when we consider the Pentagon's inability to track its own money. Pentagon accounting has been called 'frequently fictional', ledgers are sometimes still handwritten, and $1 billion can be a rounding error.[28] The Department of Defense remains the only federal agency unable to pass a financial audit.[29] Identifying the value of contracts received by specific companies is more difficult still because of complicated subcontracting arrangements, the use of foreign subsidiaries, frequent corporate name changes, and the general lack of corporate transparency.

Top Twenty-Five Recipients of Pentagon Contracts Abroad

Contract Awardee	Total (billions)
1. Miscellaneous Foreign Contractors	47.1
2. KBR, Inc.	44.4
3. Supreme Group	9.3
4. Agility Logistics (PWC)	9.0
5. DynCorp International	8.6
6. Fluor Intercontinental	8.6
7. ITT/Exelis, Inc.	7.4
8. BP, P.L.C.	5.6
9. Bahrain Petroleum Company	5.1
10. Abu Dhabi Petroleum Company	4.5
11. SK Corporation	3.8
12. Red Star Enterprises (Mina Corporation)	3.8
13. World Fuel Services Corporation	3.8
14. Motor Oil (Hellas), Corinth Refineries S.A.	3.7
15. Combat Support Associates Ltd.	3.8
16. Refinery Associates Texas, Inc.	3.3
17. Lockheed Martin Corporation	3.2
18. Raytheon Company	3.1
19. S-Oil Corporation (Ssangyong)	3.0
20. International Oil Trading Co./Trigeant Ltd.	2.7
21. FedEx Corporation	2.2
22. Contrack International, Inc.	2.0
23. GS/LG-Caltex (Chevron Corporation)	1.9
24. Washington Group/URS Corporation	1.6
25. Tutor Perini Corporation (Perini)	1.5
SUBTOTAL	**$201.8**
All Other Contractors	**$183.4**
TOTAL	**$385.2**

Source: http://usaspending.gov

Beyond the sheer volume of dollars, a troubling pattern emerges: the majority of benefits have gone to a relatively small group of private contractors. Almost a third of the $385 billion has gone to just ten contractors. They include scandal-prone companies like KBR, the former subsidiary of former Vice President Richard Cheney's old company Halliburton, and oil giant BP. With these and other contractors, large and small, Pentagon spending in the base world has been marked by spiralling expenditures, the growing use of contracts lacking incentives to control costs, sometimes criminal behaviour, and the repeated awarding of non-competitive sweetheart contracts to companies with histories of fraud and abuse.

Putting aside the unknown 'miscellaneous foreign contractors' topping the recipients' list, it is helpful to examine the top three named recipients in some detail.

1. KBR: Among the companies bringing home billions, the name Kellogg, Brown & Root dominates. It has almost five times the contracts of the next company on the list and is emblematic of broader problems in the contracting system.

KBR is the latest incarnation of Brown & Root, the company that started paving roads in Texas in 1919 and grew into the largest engineering and construction firm in the United States. In 1962, Halliburton, an international oil services company, bought Brown & Root. In 1995, Richard Cheney became Halliburton's president and CEO after helping jumpstart the Pentagon's ever-greater reliance on private contractors when he was President George H.W. Bush's secretary of defense. During the five years when Cheney ran the company, KBR won $2.3 billion in US military contracts (compared to $1.2 billion in the previous five years).[30]

Later, when Cheney was vice president, Halliburton and its KBR subsidiary (formed after acquiring Kellogg Industries) won by far the largest wartime contracts in Iraq and Afghanistan. It is difficult to overstate KBR's role in the two conflicts. Without its work, there might have been no wars. In 2005, Paul Cerjan, a former Halliburton vice president, explained that KBR was supporting more than 200,000 coalition forces in Iraq, providing 'anything they need to conduct the war'. That meant 'base support services, which includes all the billeting, the feeding, water supplies, sewage – anything it would take to run a city'. It also meant Army 'logistics functions, which include transportation, movement of POL [petroleum, oil, and lubricants] supplies, gas … spare parts, ammunition'.[31]

Most of KBR's contracts to support bases and troops overseas have come under the multi-billion-dollar Logistics Civilian Augmentation Program (LOGCAP). In 2001, KBR won a one-year LOGCAP contract to provide an undefined quantity and an undefined value of 'selected services in wartime'. The company subsequently enjoyed nearly eight years of work without facing a competitor's bid, thanks to a series of one-year contract extensions. By July 2011, KBR had received more than $37 billion in LOGCAP funds. KBR reflected the near tripling of Pentagon contracts issued without competitive bidding between 2001 and 2010. 'It's like a gigantic monopoly,' a representative from the watchdog group Taxpayers for Common Sense said of LOGCAP.

The work KBR performed under LOGCAP also reflected the Pentagon's frequent use of 'cost-plus' contracts. These reimburse a company for its expenses and then add a fee that is usually fixed contractually or determined by a performance evaluation board. The Congressional Research Service explains that because 'increased costs mean increased fees to the contractor', there is 'no incentive for the contractor to limit the government's costs'.[32] As one Halliburton official told a congressional committee bluntly, the company's unofficial mantra in Iraq became, 'Don't worry about price. It's 'cost-plus.''[33]

In 2009, the Pentagon's top auditor testified that KBR accounted for 'the vast majority' of wartime fraud.[34] The company has faced accusations of overcharging for everything from delivering food and fuel to providing housing for troops and base security services.[35] For its work at Camp Bondsteel in Kosovo, Halliburton/KBR paid $8 million to the government in 2006 to settle lawsuits charging double billing, inflating prices, and other fraud.[36]

After years of bad publicity, in 2007, Halliburton spun KBR off as an independent company and moved its headquarters from Houston to Dubai. Despite KBR's track record and a 2009 guilty plea for bribing Nigerian government officials to win gas contracts (for which its former CEO received prison time), the company has continued to receive massive government contracts. Its latest LOGCAP contract, awarded in 2008, could be worth up to $50 billion through to 2018. In early 2014, the Justice Department sued KBR and two subcontractors for exchanging kickbacks and filing false reimbursement claims for costs 'that allegedly were inflated, excessive or for goods and services that were grossly deficient or not provided'. The suit also charged KBR with transporting ice for troops' consumption in unsanitised trailers previously used as temporary morgues.[37]

2. Supreme Group: Next on the list is the company that has been described as the 'KBR for the Afghan War'. Supreme Group has won more than $9 billion in contracts for transporting and serving meals to troops in Afghanistan and at other bases worldwide. Another nearly $1.4 billion in fuel transportation contracts takes Supreme's total over $10 billion. The company's growth perfectly symbolises the soldiers-to-contractors shift in who peels the potatoes.[38]

Supreme was founded in 1957 by an Army veteran, Alfred Ornstein, who saw an opportunity to provide food for the hundreds of growing US bases in Germany. After expanding over several decades into the Middle East, Africa, and the Balkans, the company won multi-billion-dollar 'sole source contracts' that gave it a virtual monopoly over wartime food services in Afghanistan. In the decade since the start of the war in 2001, the company's revenues grew more than fifty-fold to $5.5 billion. Its profit margins between 2008 and 2011 ranged between 18 and 23 percent. Wartime contracts account for 90 per cent of revenues for the company, now based in Dubai (like KBR). They have made its majority owner, the founder's son, Stephen Ornstein, a billionaire.

Supreme's chief commercial officer, former Lieutenant General Robert Dail, provides a prime example of the revolving door between the Pentagon and its contractors. From August 2006 to November 2008, Dail headed the Pentagon's Defense Logistics Agency. The DLA awards the Pentagon's food contracts. In 2007, Dail presented Supreme with DLA's 'New Contractor of the Year Award'. Four months after leaving the Pentagon, he became the president of Supreme Group USA.

The Pentagon now says Supreme overbilled the military by $757 million. Others have started to scrutinise how the company won competition-free contracts and charged service fees as high as 75 per cent of costs. Supreme denies overcharging and claims the government owes it $1.8 billion. In 2013, Supreme unsuccessfully sued the Pentagon for awarding a new $10 billion Afghanistan food contract to a competitor that underbid Supreme's offer by $1.4 billion.[39]

3. Agility Logistics: After Supreme is Agility Logistics, a Kuwaiti company (formerly known as Public Warehousing Company KSC and PWC Logistics). It won multi-billion-dollar contracts to transport food to troops in Iraq. When the Pentagon decided against awarding similar contracts in Afghanistan to a single firm, Agility partnered with Supreme in exchange for a 3.5 per cent fee on revenues. Like Supreme, Agility hired a former high-ranking DLA official, Major General Dan Mongeon, as President of Defense & Government Services, US[40]. Mongeon joined the company just months after it won its second multi-billion dollar contract from DLA.

In 2009 and 2010, grand juries criminally indicted Agility for $6 billion in false claims and price manipulation.[41] In 2011, a grand jury subpoenaed Mongeon as part of investigations into new charges against Agility.[42] With the litigation ongoing, the Pentagon suspended the company and 125 related companies from receiving new contracts. Agility has filed a $225 million suit against the DLA for breach of contract. Strangely, the Army and the DLA have continued to do business with Agility, extending contracts with more than seven separate 'compelling reason' determinations.[43]

The rest of the top ten: a pattern of misconduct.

Things do not get much better farther down the list. Next come DynCorp International and Fluor Intercontinental. The two, along with KBR, won the latest LOGCAP contracts. Awarding that contract to three companies rather than one was intended to increase competition. In practice, according to the Commission on Wartime Contracting, each corporation has enjoyed a 'mini-monopoly' over logistics services in Afghanistan and other locations. DynCorp, which has also won large wartime private security contracts, has a history littered with charges of overbilling, shoddy construction, smuggling labourers onto bases, as well as sexual harassment and sex trafficking.

Although a Fluor employee pleaded guilty in 2012 to conspiring to steal and sell military equipment in Iraq, it is the only defence firm in the world to receive an 'A' on Transparency International's anti-corruption index that rates companies' efforts to fight corruption. On the other hand, number seven on the list, ITT (now Exelis), received a 'C' (along with KBR and DynCorp).[44]

The last three in the top ten are BP (which tops the Project on Government Oversight's federal contractor misconduct list) and the petroleum companies of Bahrain and the United Arab Emirates.[45] The military and its bases run on oil. The military consumed five billion gallons in fiscal year 2011 alone – more than all of Sweden.[46] In total, ten of the top twenty-five firms are oil companies, with contracts for delivering oil overseas totalling around $40 billion.

The Pentagon and the US government generally justify the use of so many contractors based on their supposed efficiency and saving taxpayer money. On average, this appears not to be the case. Research shows that contractors cost two to three times as much as a Pentagon civilian doing the same work. More than half of Army contracts go to administrative overhead rather than contract services.[47] Military comptrollers acknowledge that when it comes to the use of contractors, 'growth has been unchallenged'. 'The savings are here,' the comptrollers conclude.[48]

'Ice Cream'

At the Forward Operating Bases 2012 conference in London, the speakers included members of several NATO militaries. They were a reminder that while US companies working on US bases dominate the industry, private contractors increasingly build, run, and supply bases for the militaries of many nations, as well as for international peacekeepers and oil companies whose extraction facilities often look like military bases. Among the speakers was US Marine Corps Major Patrick Reynolds. With the help of a Marine Corps video, Reynolds talked about 'EXFOB' the Marines' experimental, energy-saving forward operating base (according to the video, EXFOB aims to help 'change the way we think about energy to maintain our lethality'). Referring to his audience, he said it is great that the 'beltway bandits' are on board with this new emphasis on energy efficiency. Reynolds ended his presentation by alerting the contractors to a list of upcoming contract opportunities. 'RFP to be posted on FEDBIZOPPS soon!' read one of his powerpoint slides (referring to the website advertising government procurement opportunities). Suddenly there was a noticeable surge in energy in the room. People sat up in their chairs, and for the first time during his presentation, many in the audience began taking notes on mostly blank notepads. 'I know you guys from the industry pay a lot to be here,' Reynolds said, so he thought it right to offer 'food for thought [to] give you something to walk away with'.

Just as tellingly as what appeared to be advance notice on government contract solicitations, Reynolds explained to the group how bases tend to expand exponentially over time. 'You start out small' with an outpost, he said, 'thinking you'll only be there for a week ... And then it's two weeks. And then it's a month. And then it's two months.' In the process, bases add facilities, food, and recreational amenities, like steak and lobster, flat screen TVs, and Internet connections. The major said he and others in the military refer to these comforts collectively as 'ice cream'. 'There's no "ice cream" out here' at a small outpost, he told the audience. 'But eventually you'll get to the point where it's out here' at a patrol base and not just as it is now at headquarters and FOBs. 'It's a building block process.' The process Major Reynolds described is precisely what happened on bases in and around Afghanistan and Iraq. According to a Congressional Research Service report, the Pentagon 'built up a far more extensive infrastructure than anticipated to support troops and equipment'. Funds for the operation and maintenance of bases (including food and amenities) grew three times as fast as the number of deployed troops would suggest.[49]

During a Q&A session, a Supreme Group representative asked Reynolds if the Marines were thinking about reducing the 'ice cream', the TVs, and the other amenities. I'd love to do that, the major replied. Is it going to happen? 'Sort of, kind of, not really.' 'Do we need ice cream? Do we need cable TVs? Do we need high speed internet and all the crap? No,' said Reynolds. 'But we have' Senators and Congressmen coming out and 'visiting their constituents and they want to help'. And then he paused before continuing, 'That's probably all I'll say on that.'

Major Reynolds politely pointed to some of the political players shaping the base world. They are just some of those who, in addition to the contractors, have benefited from the collection of bases abroad. For example, in Afghanistan and Iraq, Congress members have used base amenities as a public way to demonstrate their patriotism and support for the troops. One former soldier told me his reaction to arriving at Iraq's Camp Liberty was, 'This is awesome!' Like thousands of others, he found comfortable rooms, beds, and amenities that eventually included unrestricted Internet access (thanks to a favour from a KBR contractor). 'It was really plush,' he said. 'It was dope.' Later, he admitted, 'I felt ashamed it wasn't harder'.

The perks of overseas base life are far greater for the generals and the admirals who often enjoy personal assistants and chefs, private planes and vehicles, and other benefits. Beyond the authorized perks, there are cases like former Africa Command commander General William 'Kip' Ward. Pentagon investigators found Ward 'engaged in multiple forms of misconduct' including billing the government for hundreds of thousands of dollars of personal travel and misusing government funds on luxury hotels, five-car motorcades, and spa and shopping trips for his wife.[50] He also accepted free meals and tickets to a Broadway musical from an unnamed 'construction management, engineering, technology and energy services company' with millions in Pentagon contracts.[51]

Election Donations

In addition to illegal efforts to influence base contracting, contractors have made millions in campaign contributions to Congress members. According to the Center for Responsive Politics, individuals and PACs linked to military contractors gave more than $27 million in election donations in 2012 alone and have donated almost $200 million since 1990.[52] Most of these have gone to members of the armed services and appropriations committees in the Senate and House of Representatives. These committees have most of the authority over awarding military dollars. For the 2012 elections, for example, Virginia-based DynCorp's political action committee donated $10,000 to both the chair and ranking member of the House Armed Services Committee, and made additional donations to thirty-three other members of the House and Senate armed services committees and sixteen members of the two appropriations committees.[53]

Contractors also pay lobbyists millions more to sway military budgeteers and policymakers. In 2001 alone, ten leading military contractors spent more than $32 million on lobbying.[54] KBR and Halliburton spent nearly $5.5 million on lobbying between 2002 and 2012.[55] This included $420,000 in 2008 when KBR won the latest LOGCAP contract, and $620,000 the following year when it protested being barred from bidding on contracts in Kuwait.[56] Supreme spent $660,000 on lobbying in 2012 alone.[57] Agility spent $200,000 in 2011, after its second indictment on fraud charges.[58] Fluor racked up nearly $9.5 million in lobbying fees from 2002 to 2012.[59]

Even the German state of Rheinland-Pfalz lobbies the US government to keep bases in its state. Rheinland-Pfalz (also called Rhineland-Palatinate) has been home to more US troops and bases than any other. Since 2007, the state made 258 documented contacts with US government officials. Many of the contacts were with staffers, but others were with powerful Congress members with influence over bases and military policy, including Senators John Warner, Lindsey Graham, James Inhofe, and Representative Solomon Ortiz. Other meetings were with high-ranking Pentagon officials and an assistant secretary of the Army. During this period, Rheinland-Pfalz paid the high-profile Washington DC lobbying firm DLA Piper at least $772,000 to lobby on its behalf.[60] In neighbouring Baden-Württemberg, the German city of Heidelberg enlisted another prominent lobbyist, Patton Boggs, to help keep the Army in its city.[61] One sees how politicians in many countries, along with contractors, trade associations, lobbyists, Pentagon officials, military personnel, veterans, and others are deeply invested in maintaining the base status quo.

Avoiding Taxes

While contractors have enjoyed billions in taxpayer funds, many have sought to minimise US taxes paid on those profits by both legal and illegal means. Across the entire aerospace and military industry, the effective tax rate was 10.6 per cent as of 2010 (compared to the top federal statutory corporate tax rate of 35 per cent and an average effective tax rate for large profitable US companies of 12.6 per cent).⁶² In 2004, the Government Accountability Office found that 27,100 Pentagon contractors (about one in nine) were illegally evading taxes while still receiving money from government contracts. Privacy rules prevented the government from naming names, but in one case a contractor providing base services owed almost $10 million in taxes while still receiving $3.5 million from the Pentagon. The government estimated the total taxes owed at $3 billion.⁶³

In recent years, major military contractors have also increasingly created foreign-chartered subsidiaries to lower their taxes legally. At bases overseas, foreign companies frequently receive a significant proportion of base contracts, meaning these contractors pay little if any US taxes at all. Some US companies have taken advantage of this situation by creating foreign subsidiaries to do much of the work on base contracts abroad. KBR, for example, has avoided paying taxes on contracts in Iraq by using shell companies in the Cayman Islands that exist only as a name in a computer file. The company technically hired more than 21,000 of its employees with two Cayman subsidiaries, allowing it to avoid paying Social Security, Medicare, and Texas unemployment taxes. KBR officials claimed the practice saved the military money. While the practice allows the Pentagon to save money, a *Boston Globe* investigation found the loophole 'results in a significantly greater loss in revenue to the government as a whole' while giving KBR a competitive advantage over competitor companies not using the loophole. In effect, the loophole lowered KBR's contributions to the Social Security and Medicare trust funds and meant that employees could not receive unemployment benefits if they lost their jobs because they were technically employed by a foreign corporation. Robert McIntyre, the director of the advocacy group Citizens for Tax Justice, told the *Globe*, 'The argument that by not paying taxes they are saving the government money is just absurd'.⁶⁴

Similarly, while KBR's former parent Halliburton was spinning off KBR as a separate company in 2007, Halliburton announced it would move its corporate headquarters to the no-tax jurisdiction of Dubai in the United Arab Emirates (UAE) where there is no corporate income tax and no tax on employee income (Halliburton already had seventeen foreign subsidiaries in tax-haven countries). Although the company has remained legally incorporated in the United States, moving top executives to Dubai likely allowed the executives to avoid income taxes and Halliburton to avoid employee payroll taxes and reduce its corporate taxes by arguing that a portion of its global profits are attributable to work performed in Dubai, not the United States.⁶⁵

Generally under US tax law, a US firm with overseas operations can indefinitely postpone paying domestic corporate tax on its foreign income by conducting its foreign operations through a foreign-chartered subsidiary. As long as the company's foreign earnings remain under the control of the subsidiary and are reinvested abroad, US corporate income taxes are 'deferred'. The firm pays US taxes on the overseas earnings of the subsidiary only when the parent company 'repatriates' the earnings from the foreign subsidiary as intra-firm dividends or other income.[66] According to a 2012 J P Morgan study, US multinational firms have over $1.7 trillion in foreign earnings 'parked' overseas and thus shielded from U.S taxes.[67]

During a Government Accountability Office investigation, major military contractors admitted, 'the use of offshore subsidiaries in foreign jurisdictions helps them lower their US taxes. For example, one defence contractor's offshore subsidiary structure decreased its effective US tax rate by approximately 1 per cent, equalling millions of dollars in tax savings.' (Foreign subsidiaries also protect companies from some legal liabilities and potential lawsuits.)[68]

Because US corporations are taxed only when they repatriate such earnings, the current tax system encourages companies to earn and then keep their income overseas.[69] This Congressionally enacted structural incentive applies to all industries; however, its significance extends far beyond lost tax revenues in the case of contractors doing work on US bases overseas. Given equivalent contracts to provide construction or maintenance services on a base in Texas and a base in the United Arab Emirates, for example, the base in the UAE offers more options for indefinitely reducing US taxes. In short, the US tax code encourages contractors to support the stationing of bases and troops abroad.

A Self-licking Ice Cream Cone

As the FOB2012 conference neared its end, I asked another conference attendee (who asked that I not use his name) if during his wartime deployments in Iraq he had seen the problem Major Elliott had described of a base with private security guards protecting privately contracted cooks, who were cooking for the same private security guards, who were protecting the privately contracted cooks. 'A lot,' he replied. It's the 'self-licking ice cream cone' – by which he meant a self-perpetuating system with no purpose or function except to keep itself going. 'I sat with my ice cream and my prime rib on Sundays' in Iraq, he continued. It's been this way since 2001 and maybe even Kosovo. There's been lots of waste and inefficiency. Maybe, he said of the 'loggies' – the logisticians who coordinate all the 'ice cream' – it would be better 'to fire the lot and start over'.

In one of the conference's final conversations, contractor and military representatives discussed fears about the military market drying up as US and European governments cut military budgets. Contractors, many agreed, would increasingly move to build, supply, and maintain bases for UN and other international peacekeepers, as well as for oil and mining companies. Peter Eberle, a representative from General Dynamics (which just missed making the top twenty-five overseas contract recipients), asked, 'What if we have peace break out' after the US withdrawal from Afghanistan? 'God forbid!' replied Major Elliott.

Notes
1. IQPC, 'Forward Operating Bases 2012' and 'Sponsorship Opportunities,' http://iqpc.com.
2. Parts of this article stem from my article, 'Where Has All the Money Gone? How Contractors Raked in $385 Billion to Build and Support Bases Abroad since 2001,' *Tom Dispatch*, May 14, 2013, http://tomdispatch.com, and my forthcoming book *Base Nation: How American Military Bases Abroad Are Damaging National Security and Hurting Us All* (New York: Metropolitan Books, 2015). Thanks to Michael Tigar, John Mage and the other editors of *MR*, Tom Engelhardt, Clifford Rosky, Laura Jung, all those who generously offered their time and insights during interviews, and many, many others for their help with the work leading to this article.
3. David de Jong, email to author, February 4, 2014, quoting a press officer for the Secretary of Defense: 'Using October 2011 as a benchmark we had about 800 facilities – ranging from very small checkpoints that have maybe a squad or platoon of ISAF forces on it to bases that have several hundred to as many as a thousand ISAF members on them.'
4. Nick Turse, 'Afghanistan's Base Bonanza,' September 4, 2012, http://tomdispatch.com.
5. By the Pentagon's last reported count, as of September 2012, the military occupies 695 'base sites' outside the fifty states and Washington, D.C. See U.S. Department of Defense, 'Base Structure Report Fiscal Year 2013 Baseline (A Summary of DoD's Real Property Inventory),' report, Washington, DC, 2013, http://acq.osd.mil. However, this total excludes numerous well-known bases, like those in Kuwait and Afghanistan; secret bases, like those reported in Israel; and a growing number of small 'cooperative security locations' or 'lily pad' bases in Africa, Asia, and Latin American. My estimate of 800 thus is an adjustment to the Pentagon's enumeration.
6. James R. Blaker, *United States Overseas Basing: An Anatomy of the Dilemma* (New York: Praeger, 1990), 9; Tom Engelhardt, 'Advice to a Young Builder in

Tough Times: Imperial Opportunities Abound,' November 4, 2007, http://tomdispatch.com.

7 John Bellamy Foster, Harry Magdoff, and Robert W. McChesney, 'U.S. Military Bases and Empire,' *Monthly Review* 53, no. 10 (March 2002): 13. See also Chalmers Johnson, *The Sorrows of Empire: Militarism, Secrecy, and the End of the Republic* (New York: Metropolitan Books, 2004); Sydney Lens, *Permanent War: The Militarization of America* (New York: Schocken Books, 1987); Michael S. Sherry, *In the Shadows of War: The United States since the 1930s* (New Haven, CT: Yale University Press, 1995); Tom Engelhardt, 'Twenty-first Century Gunboat Diplomacy,' March 30, 2004, http://tomdispatch.com.

8 See David Vine, *Island of Shame: The Secret History of the U.S. Military Base on Diego Garcia* (Princeton: Princeton University Press, 2009).

9 Commission on Wartime Contracting in Iraq and Afghanistan, 'Transforming Wartime Contracting: Controlling Costs, Reducing Risks,' final report to Congress, August 2011, http://cybercemetery.unt.edu.

10 David Cay Johnston, 'The U.S. Government Is Paying Through the Nose for Private Contractors,' *Newsweek*, December 12, 2012, http://newsweek.com.

11 Blaker, *United States Overseas Basing*, 9.

12 U.S. Department of Defense, 'Base Structure Report.'

13 What constitutes a 'base' is a complicated question. Definitions and terminology (base, post, station, fort, installation, etc.) vary considerably. The Pentagon's annual 'Base Structure Report,' which provides an annual accounting of its facilities and from which I derive the estimate of 800, refers to 'base sites' (see note 5). In some cases, this means that an installation generally referred to as a single base (like Aviano Air Base in Italy) actually consists of multiple distinct base sites – in Aviano's case, at least eight. For counting purposes, however, it makes sense to follow the Pentagon's lead, given that base sites with the same name can often be in geographically disparate locations. Generally too, each site represents a distinct Congressional appropriation of taxpayer funds. To avoid the linguistic debates, however, and because it's the simplest and most widely recognized name, I use 'base' – taken to mean any structure, facility, or place regularly used for military purposes of any kind (see Blaker, *United States Overseas Basing*, 4).

14 Catherine Lutz, in Catherine Lutz, ed., 'Introduction: Bases, Empire, and Global Response,' *The Bases of Empire: The Global Struggle against U.S. Military Posts* (New York: NYU Press, 2009), 4.

15 U.S. Department of Defense, 'Base Structure Report,' 2-8; Dan Burrows, 'Planet Walmart: Five Big Facts About the World's Largest Company,' October 13, 2010, http://dailyfinance.com/; McDonald's Corporation, 'Getting to Know Us,' http://aboutmcdonalds.com; U.S. Department of State, accessed January 15, 2014, http://usembassy.gov.

16 See David Vine, 'Picking Up a $170 Billion Tab: How U.S. Taxpayers Are

Paying the Pentagon to Occupy the Planet,' December 11, 2012, http://tomdispatch.com.
17 Pratap Chatterjee, *Halliburton's Army: How a Well-Connected Texas Oil Company Revolutionized the Way America Makes War* (New York: Nation Books, 2009), 24–27.
18 Ibid, 18–20.
19 P.W. Singer, *Corporate Warriors: The Rise of the Privatized Military Industry* (Ithaca: Cornell University Press, 2003), 80.
20 Chatterjee, *Halliburton's Army*, 61-62.
21 Ibid, 214.
22 Guy Raz, 'U.S. Builds Air Base in Iraq for Long Haul,' *All Things Considered*, October 12, 2007, http://npr.org; Engelhardt, 'Advice to a Young Builder.'
23 Commission on Wartime Contracting in Iraq and Afghanistan, 'Transforming Wartime Contracting,' 208–210.
24 Linda Bilmes, 'Who Profited from the Iraq War,' *EPS Quarterly* 24, no. 1 (March 2012): 6, http://epsusa.org. The Federal Procurement Data System that's supposed to track government contracts 'often contains inaccurate data,' according to the Government Accountability Office, 'Federal Contracting: Observations on the Government's Contracting Data Systems,' report, GAO-09-1032T, September 29, 2009, http://gao.gov. For example, my research showed hundreds of thousands of contracts with no 'place of performance' listed. On the other hand, there were 116,527 contracts listing the place of performance as Switzerland, even though the vast majority of the contracts are for delivering food to troops in Afghanistan and at bases worldwide (one of the major companies providing food, an arm of Supreme Group, is based in Switzerland).
25 See e.g., Wilson Andrews and Todd Lindeman, 'The Black Budget,' *Washington Post,* August 29, 2013, http://washingtonpost.com.
26 Or various iterations of the same term.
27 Commission on Wartime Contracting in Iraq and Afghanistan, 'Transforming Wartime Contracting,' 209.
28 R. Jeffrey Smith, 'Pentagon's Accounting Shambles May Cost an Additional $1 Billion,' *Center for Public Integrity*, October 13, 2011 (updated, March 23, 2012), http://publicintegrity.org.
29 Asif A. Khan, 'DOD Financial Management: Weaknesses in Controls over the Use of Public Funds and Related Improper Payments,' United States Government Accountability Office testimony, Panel on Defense Financial Management and Auditability Reform, Committee on Armed Services, House of Representatives, September 22, 2011, http://gao.gov.
30 Chatterjee, *Halliburton's Army*, 49.
31 Ibid, 9.
32 Valerie B. Grosso, 'Defense Contracting in Iraq: Issues and Options for Congress,' Congressional Research Service, Washington, DC, June 18, 2008,

http://fpc.state.gov.
33 United States House of Representatives Committee on Oversight and Government Reform, 'It's Your Money: Iraq Reconstruction,' http://oversight-archive.waxman.house.gov.
34 Ellen Nakashima, 'KBR Connected to Alleged Fraud, Pentagon Auditor Says,' *Washington Post,* May 5, 2009, http://washingtonpost.com.
35 Dana Hedgpeth, 'Audit of KBR Iraq Contract Faults Records For Fuel, Food,' *Washington Post,* June 25, 2007, http://washingtonpost.com; U.S. Department of Justice, Office of Public Affairs, 'United States Sues Houston-based KBR and Kuwaiti Subcontractor for False Claims on Contracts to House American Troops in Iraq,' press release, November 19, 2012, http://justice.gov/opa/pr; Walter Pincus, 'U.S. Files Civil Suit Against Defense Contractor KBR,' April 2, 2010, *Washington Post,* http://washingtonpost.com.
36 Chatterjee, *Halliburton's Army,* 63–64.
37 U.S. Department of Justice, Office of Public Affairs, 'United States Government Sues Kellogg, Brown & Root Services Inc. and Two Foreign Companies for Kickbacks and False Claims Relating to Iraq Support Services Contract,' press release, January 23, 2014, http://justice.gov/opa/pr.
38 The best source for this section is David de Jong, 'Supreme Owner Made a Billionaire Feeding U.S. War Machine,' *Bloomberg,* October 7, 2013, http://bloomberg.com.
39 Andrew Zajac, 'Supreme Foodservice Sues Over U.S., Afghan Food Contract,' *Bloomberg News,* April 8, 2013, http://bloomberg.com. See also Supreme Foodservice, GmbH v. United States, No. 13-245 C (September 18, 2013).
40 Walter Pincus, 'Agency Extends Afghan Food-Supply Contract for Firm that Hired Former Director,' *Washington Post,* January 4, 2011, http://washingtonpost.com.
41 Neil Gordon, 'Pentagon Ordered to Lift Suspension of Kuwaiti Contractor's Affiliates,' *Project On Government Oversight (POGO) Blog,* July 3, 2012, http://pogoblog.typepad.com.
42 David Beasley, 'Agility Prosecutors Probing 'Potential New Charges' in U.S., Judge Writes,' *Bloomberg News,* July 27, 2011, http://bloomberg.com.
43 Neil Gordon, 'POGO Obtains Second Helping of 'Compelling Reason' Memos,' *POGO Blog,* October 9, 2013, http://pogo.org.
44 Project on Government Oversight (POGO), 'Fluor Corporation,' Federal Contractor Misconduct Database, http://contractormisconduct.org; Transparency International UK, 'Defence Companies Anti-Corruption Index 2012,' report, London, October 2012, http://companies.defenceindex.org/report.
45 Project on Government Oversight (POGO), 'Top 100 Contractors,' Federal Contractor Misconduct Database, http://contractormisconduct.org.
46 U.S. Department of Defense, 'Department of Defense Annual Energy Management Report Fiscal Year 2011,' report, September 2012; U.S. Energy

Information Administration, Countries, n.d. [2013], http://eia.gov/countries.
47 Johnston, 'The U.S. Government Is Paying Through the Nose for Private Contractors.'
48 American Society of Military Comptrollers, 'Service Support Contractors: One of the FY 2012 Budget Efficiencies,' powerpoint presentation, Department of Defense, October 2011, http://asmconline.org.
49 Amy Belasco, 'The Cost of Iraq, Afghanistan, and Other Global War on Terror Operations Since 9/11,' Congressional Research Service, report, Washington, DC, March 29, 2011, 38, http://asmconline.org.
50 Inspector General United States Department of Defense, 'Report of Investigation: United States Army General William E. Ward, U.S. Army Commander, U.S. AFRICOM,' report, Alexandria, VA, June 26, 2012, http://wired.com.
51 Spencer Ackerman, 'Top General Undone by Spa Treatments, Snickers, Broadway Show,' August 17, 2012, http://wired.com.
52 Center for Responsive Politics, 'Defense,' http://opensecrets.org.
53 Center for Responsive Politics, 'DynCorp International, Expenditures' http://opensecrets.org; 'DynCorp International, Recipients,' http://opensecrets.org.
54 David Isenberg, *Shadow Force: Private Security Contractors in Iraq* (Westport, CT: Praeger Security International, 2009), 65.
55 Center for Responsive Politics, 'Halliburton Co., Profile: Summary, 2012 Summary,' http://opensecrets.org.
56 Government Accountability Office, 'Decision in the Matter of Kellogg Brown & Root Services, Inc.,' File: B-400787.2; B-400861, Washington, DC, February 23, 2009, http://gao.gov.
57 Center for Responsive Politics, 'Supreme Group USA, Summary,' http://opensecrets.org.
58 Center for Responsive Politics, 'Agility Public Warehousing Co, Summary,' http://opensecrets.org.
59 Center for Responsive Politics, 'Fluor Corp, Summary,' http://opensecrets.org.
60 Sunlight Foundation, 'German State of Rheinland-Pfalz,' http://foreign.influenceexplorer.com.
61 AALEP, 'EU Member States' Lobbying in the U.S.,' list from Foreign Agent Registration Act's Report, December 31, 2010, [2011], http://aalep.eu, 6; Sunlight Foundation, 'The City of Heidelberg, Germany,' http://foreign.influenceexplorer.com.
62 Robert S. McIntyre, Matthew Gardner, Rebecca J. Wilkins, and Richard Phillips, 'Corporate Taxpayers & Corporate Tax Dodgers 2008–10,' report, Institute on Taxation and Economic Policy, November 2011, http://ctj.org, 8; U.S. Government Accountability Office, 'Corporate Income Tax: Effective Tax Rates Can Differ Significantly from the Statutory Rate,' report to Congress, GAO-13-520, Washington, DC, May 2013, http://gao.gov.
63 Robert D. Hershey Jr., 'Tax Questions For Military's Contractors,' *New York*

Times, February 12, 2004, http://nytimes.com.
64 Farah Stockman, 'Top Iraq Contractor Skirts U.S. Taxes with Offshore Shell Companies,' *Boston Globe,* March 9, 2008, E7. A 2008 change in U.S. tax law closed the loophole that allowed companies to avoid paying Social Security and Medicare taxes but left the loophole intact for unemployment taxes, meaning that former employees remain ineligible for unemployment insurance. Government Accountability Office, 'Defense Contracting: Recent Law Has Impacted Contractor Use of Offshore Subsidiaries to Avoid Certain Payroll Taxes,' Highlights of GAO-10-327, Washington, DC, January 2010, http://gao.gov.
65 Chatterjee, *Halliburton's Army*, 210–11; Laura Mandaro, 'Halliburton's Dubai Move Raises Issue of Expat Taxes,' March 13, 2007, http://marketwatch.com.
66 Congressional Research Service, 'Tax Exemption for Repatriated Foreign Earnings: Proposals and Analysis,' Report for Congress, Washington, DC, April 27, 2006, http://congressionalresearch.com.
67 Senate Republican Policy Committee, 'Territorial vs. Worldwide Taxation,' September 19, 2012, http://rpc.senate.gov; Emily Chasan, 'At Big U.S. Companies, 60% of Cash Sits Offshore: J.P. Morgan,' W*all Street Journal,* May 17, 2012, http://blogs.wsj.com.
68 United States Government Accountability Office, 'Defense Contracting: Recent Law.'
69 Senate Republican Policy Committee, 'Territorial vs. Worldwide Taxation.'

mrzine.monthlyreview.org

Russell Tribunal on Palestine Jurors

Pierre Galand, who initiated the Russell Tribunal on Palestine

Diego Garcia

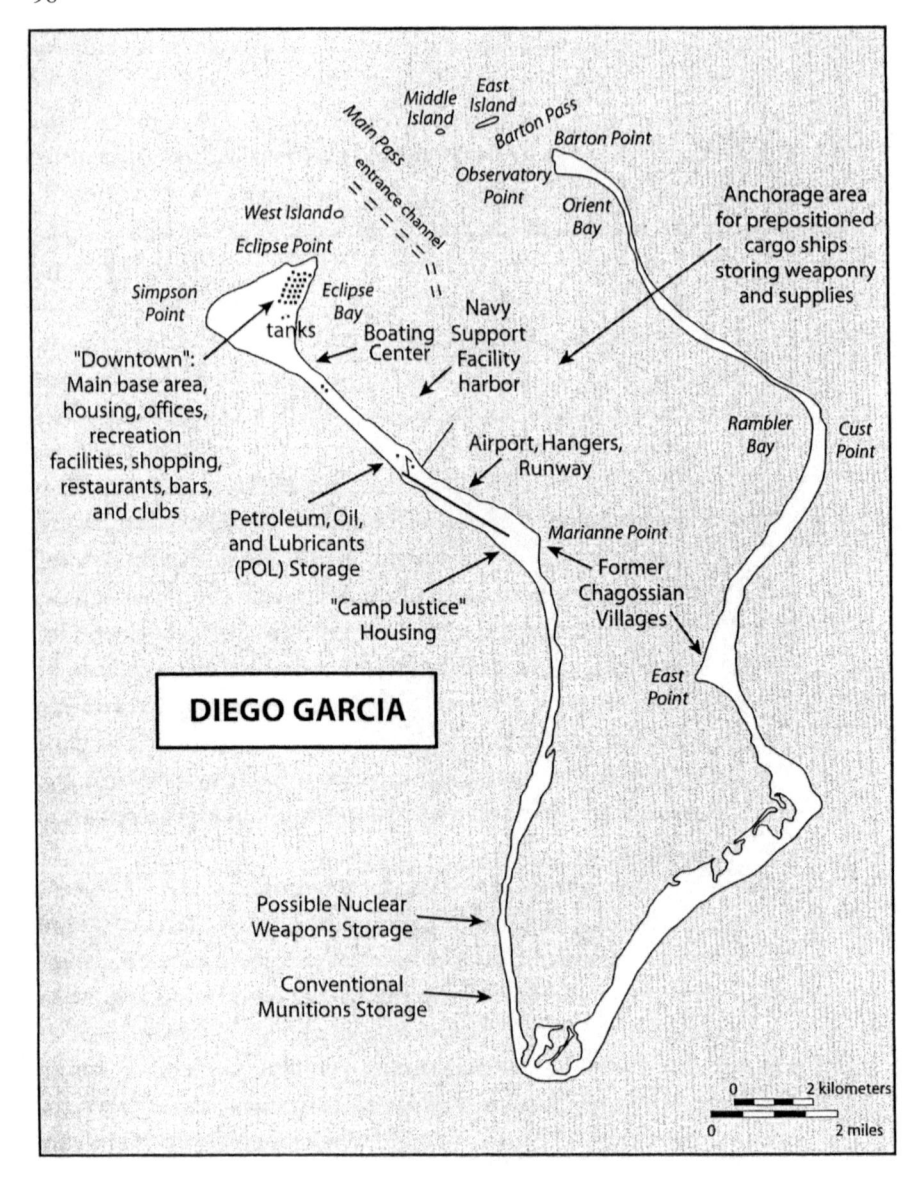

Map labels:
- Middle Island
- East Island
- Main Pass
- Barton Pass
- Barton Point
- Observatory Point
- Orient Bay
- Anchorage area for prepositioned cargo ships storing weaponry and supplies
- West Island
- Eclipse Point
- entrance channel
- Simpson Point
- Eclipse Bay
- tanks
- Boating Center
- Navy Support Facility harbor
- "Downtown": Main base area, housing, offices, recreation facilities, shopping, restaurants, bars, and clubs
- Airport, Hangers, Runway
- Rambler Bay
- Cust Point
- Petroleum, Oil, and Lubricants (POL) Storage
- Marianne Point
- Former Chagossian Villages
- "Camp Justice" Housing
- East Point
- Possible Nuclear Weapons Storage
- Conventional Munitions Storage
- 0   2 kilometers
- 0   2 miles

Running the planet from Diego Garcia

"'It's the single most important military facility we've got,' respected Washington-area military expert John Pike told me. Pike, who runs the website GlobalSecurity.org, explained, "It's the base from which we control half of Africa and the southern side of Asia, the southern side of Eurasia." It's "the facility that at the end of the day gives us some say-so in the Persian Gulf region. If it didn't exist, it would have to be invented." The base is critical to controlling not just the oil-rich Gulf but the world, said Pike: "Even if the entire Eastern Hemisphere has drop-kicked us" from every other base on their territory, he explained, the military's goal is to be able "to run the planet from Guam and Diego Garcia by 2015.'"

Full Spectrum Dominance, which used to be the declared military doctrine of the United States (see *Spokesman 71, Will America Die of Defence?*), has suffered serial reality checks, in Afghanistan, Iraq, Libya, and elsewhere. But the mindset endures, as John Pike reveals in his candid remarks about Guam and Diego Garcia to David Vine, recorded in *Island of Shame*. With an anthropologist's sensitivity, Vine records the experiences of some 1,300 Chagossians who were forcibly expelled from their homes on the Indian Ocean island of Diego Garcia in the 1960s, where their families had lived since the eighteenth century (see map). The British did the dirty work of expulsion (very badly), while the United States pulled the strings. The Brits were broke and retreating from east of Suez. Meanwhile, busy in Vietnam, but always mindful of its Cold War opponent, the US military was developing a 'strategic island concept', whereby it established naval and air facilities at strategic locations, which, in the case of Diego Garcia, was convenient for policing the oil-rich yet turbulent Middle East. The US insisted the island be cleansed of its indigenous population. In exchange for its co-operation, Britain received a £5 million discount on its share of the bill for developing the Polaris nuclear weapon system. UK Parliamentary scrutiny was avoided by invoking the royal prerogative, while UN displeasure at the dismembering of Mauritius (of which the Chagos Archipelago was part) was largely disregarded. Down the decades, the Chagossians continued their legal struggle to return home, with some notable successes. Professor Vine tells this story of our times in lucid detail, with great authority, and sustained empathy for the victims.

Tony Simpson

David Vine, Island of Shame: The secret history of the US military base on Diego Garcia, Princeton University Press, 2009, ISBN 9780691149837, £16.95

INSULTING MACHINES

It is a graceful degradation, bristling with paths not taken
Supercharged by Taylor's one best way
with all the zeal of the monotheist
Where Schumpeter shoves, Kondratiev waves and Gladwell points
All in hot pursuit of singularity.
Behold the strange phyla as they stalk their makers
They too can walk, feed, talk and – some say – think.

We create devices and then they create us.
Narcissus-like, we gaze into a pool of technology and see ourselves.
We acquiesce in our own demise, setting out as participants
and metamorphosing into victims.
The diagnosis is serious: a rapidly spreading species' loss of nerve
Tacit knowledge is demeaned whilst propositional knowledge is revered.
Who needs imagination when there are facts?

A human enhancing symbiosis ignored
whilst a dangerous convergence proceeds apace – as human beings
confer life on machines and in so doing diminish themselves.

Your calculus may be greater than his calculus
but will it pass the Sullenberger Hudson River test?
Meantime, the virtual is confused with the real
– as parents lavish attention on the virtual child
whilst their real child dies of neglect and starvation.

Potential and reality are torn apart as change is confused with progress
With slender knowledge of deep subjects
– you proceed with present tense technology,
obliterating the past and with the future already mortgaged.
The court of history may find you intoxicated with species arrogance
recklessly proceeding without a Hippocratic Oath.

Thus the deskiller is deskilled, as a tsunami of technology
rocks our foundations.
The multinational apologist solemnly declares: 'We should have the courage
to accept our true place in the evolutionary hierarchy
– namely animals, humans and post singularity systems'.
Now the sky darkens with pigeons coming home to roost
and the mine canaries topple from their perches unnoticed.

That distant sound grows louder.
Is it the life affirming energy of Riverdance
or the clacking hooves of the Four Horsemen?
That music, is it 'Ode to Joy' or is it 'Twilight of the Gods?'
As the embrace tightens into genteel strangulation – will the seducer
in final deception whisper 'Shall I compare thee to a Summer's day?'

Mike Cooley

This poem was first published in AI & SOCIETY Vol.28 No.4 Dec 2013.

Chrome Dome

Ray Perkins, Jr

The author is Emeritus Professor of Philosophy at Plymouth State University. He is vice-president of the Bertrand Russell Society, from which he received the 2002 Book Award for Yours Faithfully, Bertrand Russell. *With grateful acknowledgements to him and Kenneth Blackwell, editor of* Russell: the journal of Bertrand Russell Studies, *where this review article first appeared.*

Eric Schlosser. Command and Control: Nuclear Weapons, the Damascus Accident and the Illusion of Safety, *Penguin Allen Lane, 2013, 656 pages, 9781846141485, £25*

Eric Schlosser has given us a very important and much needed look at the history of US nuclear weapons safety. The book is well researched and, despite its subtitle, is more than a history of nuclear weapons safety. In the course of developing his thesis that nuclear weapons have been – and continue to be – a shockingly dangerous part of the post-World War Two world, we get not only a tutorial on nuclear weapons and delivery systems, but a fascinating and eye-opening account of the dynamic of the nuclear arms race, replete with inter-service rivalries, ideological fanaticism, and the struggle for civilian control. It was this dynamic which gave us obscenely bloated nuclear arsenals and a military leadership that too often favoured weapons reliability over safety.

The story is cogently covered in the course of recounting in considerable detail what has to be one of the most frightening of US nuclear weapons accidents (and there were hundreds[1]) – viz. the 18 September 1980 accident in Damascus, Arkansas involving a Titan II inter-continental ballistic missile with a nine-megaton warhead.[2] During a check for a possible fuel system leak, a mechanic near the top of the missile (in a hardened silo beneath ground) dropped a nine-pound wrench socket which fell 70 feet and punctured the fuel tank; eight hours later, despite efforts to contain highly flammable fuel vapours, the missile exploded, covering the complex in a huge fireball and toxic gases. The warhead, the largest in the US arsenal at the time, was catapulted 1,000 feet into the air and landed a quarter mile away, largely intact. By good luck (and the grace of God?)[3], there was no thermonuclear detonation – especially fortuitous since the warhead had long been identified by its designer (Sandia Laboratory) as one of the least safe in the US arsenal, i.e. one of the most likely to detonate in 'abnormal environments' (such as intense heat). Sandia had petitioned the Pentagon for more than a decade to retire or retrofit the warhead (p.334).

The Damascus incident concerns, directly or indirectly, most of the book. But the story is told rivetingly with many detours into weapons history, technical information, and a cast of interviewees connected with the nuclear military-industrial complex at various levels. One of Schlosser's most important characters, and from whom he gets much of his information, is Bob Peurifoy, a longtime nuclear weapons engineer and vice-president at Sandia who waged an heroic thirty-year campaign against Pentagon resistance to nuclear weapons safety. With the help of the Freedom of Information Act and recently declassified material, Schlosser provides the reader with literally scores of examples of terrifying nuclear accidents, including events that could easily have led to nuclear war. In the interests of time and space I'll briefly describe only a few.[4]

- 1961 (Jan. 23) near Goldsboro, North Carolina. A B-52 on airborne alert[5] carrying two four-megaton bombs collided with a refuelling tanker causing the B-52 to break apart and lose both bombs. One fell freely into a swamp burying itself in 70 feet of mud. Its uranium core was never found. The other descended by parachute, but electrical crystals in its nose were crushed on impact, sending a signal to detonate. All but one of three safety mechanisms failed. (pp.245–7.)
- 1965 (Aug. 9) near Searcy, Arkansas. A flash fire in a Titan II missile silo burned for ten hours, killing 53 workers and narrowly avoiding ignition of the missile fuel. (pp.23–7.)
- 1966 (Jan. 17) near Palomares, Spain. A B-52 on a Chrome Dome[6] mission carrying four one-megaton bombs collided with a refuelling tanker and crashed. Three bombs were found the next day, one largely intact, but the conventional explosives[7] of the other two had detonated, scattering plutonium and bomb fragments over large sections of Palomares. The fourth H-bomb was found two months later a mile off the coast and recovered in 2,000 feet of water. (pp.315–19.)
- 1968 (Jan. 21) near Thule, Greenland. A B-52 on a Chrome Dome mission (carrying four one-megaton bombs) to monitor the ballistic missile early warning system at Thule caught fire (a co-pilot's seating cushion blocked a hot air vent) and crashed. The H-bombs' conventional explosives, as well as 100 tons of jet fuel, exploded on impact scattering bits of plutonium over three square miles. The airborne alert programme

was finally cancelled.[8] (pp.319–25.)
- 1980 (June 3) at NORAD (North American Air Defense Command) headquarters in Cheyenne Mountain, Colorado. Computers showed a Soviet missile attack. This was a time of considerable international tension (recent Soviet invasion of Afghanistan, US hostages in Iran, US boycott of Moscow Olympics). President Carter's foreign policy advisor (Z. Brzezinski) was awakened at 2:30 a.m. and informed by his military assistant (General Odom) that 2,200 Soviet sub-launched missiles were on their way. Strategic Air Command bases nationwide – bomber and missile crews – were put on high alert. The airborne command post of the Pacific Command took off. About the time the president was being contacted, a false alarm was declared due to computer error; a defective 46-cent computer chip was later identified as the cause. (pp.367–8.)

Schlosser reveals many such disturbingly close calls to nuclear war. Since the end of the Cold War it's become fairly well known that the US and USSR came very close to war during the Cuban Missile Crisis. President Kennedy's top military advisers – including chair of the Joint Chiefs, Maxwell Taylor – urged Kennedy to attack Cuba and destroy the missiles. Even Secretary of Defense McNamara urged a limited strike. But unknown to them, the Soviets had – apart from their medium/intermediate range missiles – about 100 tactical nuclear weapons on the island, some with the force yield of the Hiroshima bomb, and with pre-delegated authority for use in case of attack. Almost certainly a US invasion would have triggered a nuclear war (pp.290–4).

Less well known is the close call the year before – the 1961 Berlin Crisis which was critical for at least two months (mid-September to late November). President Kennedy said the West will 'defend ... their access to West Berlin ... by whatever means ...'; and McNamara made clear that NATO would use nuclear weapons 'whenever we feel it necessary to protect our vital interests' (p.284). In fact, given the Warsaw Pact's conventional force superiority, there seems to have been a NATO consensus that nukes would be required should fighting break out. A main question was whether their use should follow the official plan (SIOP)[9] whereby at least 100 million Soviets would be killed in a counter-value (counter-city) attack, or a more 'moral' surprise attack (counterforce decapitation) taking 'only' a million lives. Kennedy apparently favoured the latter, but was informed that a Soviet retaliation killing five to thirteen million Americans couldn't be ruled out. There were several exacerbating events at this time: American and Soviet tanks were face to face at Checkpoint Charlie; NATO commanders had received pre-delegated emergency nuclear authority; NATO troops had 'Davy Crockett' nuclear rifles; the Soviets ended the nuclear test moratorium by exploding a 50-megaton bomb; and, at the height of the crisis in November, a faulty AT&T switch at NORAD headquarters in Colorado caused Strategic Air Command in Omaha to lose communication with the early warning system at Thule, resulting in a world-wide SAC alert and orders to hundreds of aircraft to prepare for takeoff. Luckily, the order was soon rescinded when B-52s on airborne alert around Thule reported no sign of a Soviet surprise attack (p.286).

While reading Schlosser's account of the Cold War nuclear madness – many of the particulars being unknown until recently – it occurred to me how remarkably insightful Bertrand Russell's nuclear warnings were in the late 1950s and early 1960s. Russell was, as we know, highly suspicious of official propaganda, and was a careful reader of the Western press. He was also well enough connected with experts in the field (e.g., through the Pugwash Movement) to have gained a clear picture of the nature and gravity of the nuclear peril. Moreover, he had the moral courage to publicly challenge the status quo, often in the face of hostile criticism, especially in the US media.[10] Schlosser's book is a vindication of much of Russell's anti-nuclear message, often unfairly characterised as alarmist. We now know, thanks in part to Schlosser's research, that Russell's nuclear fears and warnings were wholly justified at the time.[11]

Most of the book's horror stories took place during the Cold War when tensions ran high and both sides feared an 'out of the blue' first strike.[12] Since then stockpiles have been significantly reduced (by 80%) and long-needed safety improvements finally made. But, as Schlosser makes clear, we are not yet out of the nuclear woods. Currently the US and Russia (with 90% of the world's nuclear weapons) each have about 1,700 deployed nuclear weapons in their strategic triads (land-based missiles, sea-based missiles, and long-range bombers). Schlosser reminds us that on 25 January 1995 – several years after the end of the Cold War – a Norwegian four-stage weather rocket appeared on Russian radar to be a US Trident sub-launched missile headed for Moscow as the first of a possible surprise attack. Russian nuclear forces were put on high alert, Yeltsin was notified, and his nuclear briefcase authorising nuclear launch was activated. Fortunately, after eight minutes (of a twelve-minute limit for decision on launch), the missile was determined to be moving away from Russia, and was not a threat.[13] More than twenty years after the end of the Cold War, both sides' ICBMs (about 1,500 total) are still kept on hair-trigger alert and are ready to fire within minutes of attack warning. And both sides' ICBMs are apparently still in a 'launch on warning' posture.[14]

And, as we know, there are other nuclear problems today as well: nuclear terrorism, horizontal proliferation, and the volatility of the Pakistan-India rivalry with both nations armed with nuclear weapons and already having come close to nuclear war on a half-dozen occasions (p. 479; and see note 18).

This is a valuable book, and it should be read by all who value Bertrand Russell's vision of a world without nuclear weapons or war. But although *Command and Control* will be useful to that end, Schlosser sees himself as a 'realist' of a 'middle road' who eschews the 'idealism' of the nuclear abolitionists no less than the dangers of the counterforce advocates who favour weapons for thousands of targets. In short, he's resigned to a 'nukes forever' world in which the only acceptable nuclear strategy is the 'realistic' one of 'minimum deterrence' requiring 'only' several hundred weapons for perhaps a half dozen nations. Maybe. But there are at least two points which should give us pause.

Minimum deterrence needn't be the final step in the on-going nuclear disarmament process that began only several decades ago. It could be a penultimate step in one of several necessary steps on a road to zero – a goal that many world leaders, including the US President, have recently endorsed as both desirable and doable.[15] As Russell pointed out many years ago, *any* agreements in the arena of international security tend to diminish tensions and build confidence in the negotiation process, which in turn lead to even bolder, better agreements.[16] (We witnessed this phenomenon towards the end of the Cold War when, once the superpowers' common nuclear danger was publicly acknowledged and tensions eased, one side's arms-control proposal of unilateral cuts was met with a counter-proposal for even deeper cuts in a kind of arms race in reverse.[17] The point is, the very process of getting to minimum deterrence might well create the international machinery and climate conducive to a 'no nukes' world. I think Schlosser needs to take seriously these hopeful possibilities and developments.

Finally, the acceptance of minimum deterrence, even at the level of a few nations and a few hundred weapons, carries with it a near-certain risk of eventual nuclear disaster. But even if it didn't, minimum deterrence still comes at an unacceptably high *moral* cost: it accepts – even *requires* – the preparation for, and the willingness to commit, the killing of large numbers of innocent human beings.[18] This inherent willingness to murder – which Bertrand Russell once (at least) described as 'genocide'[19] – is a powerful component in the case against nuclear deterrence and one which Schlosser seems to dismiss as simply unworthy of the 'realist'. I think this an unfortunate shortcoming in an otherwise good book.

Notes

1 A Sandia Laboratory study found at least 1,200 'serious' accidents involving nuclear weapons between 1950 and 1968. The most serious are called 'broken arrows' in Defense Department parlance. These include unauthorized launch, release of a weapon, fire, explosion, release of radioactivity or full-scale detonation. The Department of Defence reported only a small percentage of accidents until 1959, after which they reported about 130 per year (p.327). Most of Schlosser's data on nuclear accidents – and he cites dozens of examples throughout his book – come from the declassification of DoD material since the end of the Cold War and skilful use of the Freedom of Information Act. There has long been some information regarding nuclear mishaps accessible to careful readers of the US press – to be sure only a tiny percentage, but enough to justify public concern. Bertrand Russell's was a voice that sounded early warnings based upon information that was publicly available in the late 1950s and early 60s. See note 10.
2 A nine-megaton warhead is one with a force yield the equivalent of nine million tons of TNT or approximately 600 Hiroshima bombs.
3 One reviewer of Schlosser's book (with some tongue in cheek, no doubt) takes the absence of nuclear detonation at Damascus – or in any of the hundreds of other accidents over the last 50 years – as strong evidence for the existence of a quasi-benevolent deity. See *http://www.dailykos.com/user/ATexican*. *Cf.* General Lee Butler's remark after taking charge of the Strategic Air Command in 1991 and having opportunity to study the US official nuclear war plans (i.e. the SIOP, see note 9): 'I came to fully appreciate the truth ... we escaped the Cold War without a nuclear holocaust by some combination of skill, luck, and divine intervention, and I suspect the latter in greatest proportion' (p.457).
4 Several of these accidents came to public attention at the time, although always with partial cover-up, deception and serious understatement of the public danger. But Schlosser also makes clear that there were literally hundreds that were kept secret for the duration of the Cold War, even from high-level people in the weapons factories (see p.465).
5 Airborne alert was a Strategic Air Command (SAC) practice begun in 1958 whereby a number of B-52s with thermonuclear weapons (H-bombs) would be continuously aloft and near the Soviet Union to assure retaliatory capability in the event of surprise attack. This dangerous practice lasted ten years despite a 1958 Rand study suggesting that a B-52 crashed about every 20,000 flight hours and that SAC should expect roughly twelve crashes per year (p.191).
6 Chrome Dome was an airborne alert programme which included continuous B-52 monitoring of the Mediterranean region.
7 A hydrogen bomb depends on fusion as well as fission – actually a

fission–fusion–fission sequence – to yield a nuclear explosion potentially hundreds of times greater than that of an atomic (non-thermonuclear) bomb. But the mechanism that initiates the sequence typically involves conventional high explosives.

8 Although Denmark had imposed a ban on nuclear weapons on (and over) their territory in the mid-1950s, the US had routinely violated it since 1961 with B-52 flights over Thule, and for several years before that by secretly storing nuclear weapons there for pick-up *en route* to bomb the Soviet Union (p.191).

9 The Single Integrated Operation Plan (SIOP) was the official US nuclear war plan replete with targeting details. For virtually all of the Cold War it was mechanistic, inflexible and required the use of thousands of warheads for counter-city targets assuring total destruction.

10 See Russell's debate with Edward Teller where Teller accuses Russell of 'very greatly exaggerating' the dangers of nuclear war (Edward R. Murrow's 'Small World', 28 Feb. 1960).

Cf. Russell's lengthy exchange with editor John Fischer in *Harper's Magazine*, 'Bertrand Russell on the Sinful Americans' (June 1963); reprinted in *Yours Faithfully, Bertrand Russell (ed. Ray Perkins, Jr.)*, pp.341–7. Fischer accuses him of lack of intellectual rigour and misinformation, especially on the danger of accidental nuclear war due to fallible radar and short warning time. The exchange leaves little doubt of Russell's grasp of the peril of war by miscalculation and accident. He cites a 1960 report by the Mershon Center for International Security Studies at Ohio State University, later published (1962) as *Accidental War: Some Dangers in the 1960's,* which cites many examples, and for which Russell wrote the Introduction. Perhaps the earliest example publicly mentioned by Russell (and not found in Schlosser) is a letter to *The Guardian* (30 Dec. 1960), 'Mistaken Identity at Thule', concerning an error regarding the Early Warning Ballistic Missile System at Thule, which reported that the US was under nuclear attack – the moon had been mistaken for Soviet missiles. See *Yours Faithfully*, pp.236–7.

11 Schlosser mentions Russell in several places, but fails to acknowledge his campaign to educate the public on the dangers of accidental war and his considerable influence in slowing the nuclear arms race and hastening the end of the Cold War.

He also mis-states Russell's preventive war position. Russell did *not* 'urge the Western democracies to attack the Soviet Union before it got the bomb' (p.82). And worse, he cites my 1994 *Russell* article as evidence that he did! I'm flattered. But I wish he had actually read it. See Perkins, 'Bertrand Russell's Preventive War Phase'.

12 With the advent of ICBMs, both sides secretly (and rightly) feared a surprise attack decapitating their vulnerable command and control systems, leaving them unable to respond. This was especially so with the development in the 1970s of the MIRV technology – multiple and independently targeted warheads (p.255).

13 The nuclear brief case, also called the 'nuclear football' or 'black bag',

contains the 'go codes' for launching a nuclear attack. In the US it is typically carried by an Army lieutenant colonel who accompanies the President at all times. This was apparently the first and only time the brief case has been opened and the codes retrieved in readiness for launch (p.478). See also Forrow *et al.*, 'Accidental Nuclear War – a Post-Cold War Assessment'.

14 Schlosser mentions a little-known detail about Soviet command and control. In the mid-1980s – when US officials at the highest levels were publicly proclaiming that a nuclear war could be fought and won – the Soviets, fearing command and control decapitation, implemented a version of the *Dr. Strangelove* 'doomsday machine' which they called 'Perimeter' (also 'dead hand'). In the event of attack (a confirmed impact), it would guarantee intercontinental ballistic missile retaliation without need of presidential authority, thus avoiding the need for a launch-on-warning decision with its disastrous risk of error. Schlosser misleadingly describes it as 'automatic' and 'without any human oversight'. Not quite; there were a few invulnerable technicians hidden deep underground who could, after confirmed attack, disobey the pre-set order for retaliation. This is made clear in a work that he himself cites. See Hoffman, *Dead Hand*, pp.421–3. Astonishingly (and ironically), as in *Strangelove*, it was keep secret from the US. The system was dismantled at the end of the Cold War (Schlosser, p.468).

15 One such plan, not mentioned by Schlosser, has recently been proposed by Global Zero, an international group founded in 2008, of some 300 world leaders to eliminate all nuclear weapons globally by 2030. Their 2009 plan – endorsed by more than twenty former heads of state including Vaclav Havel, Jimmy Carter, Mikhail Gorbachev and Helmut Schmidt – proposes a four-stage abolition process over 30 years. Former US senator Chuck Hagel signed the plan in 2012, the year before he became Secretary of Defense.

16 See the 'Russell-Einstein Manifesto' (1955), reprinted in *Has Man a Future?*, p.57, and *Collected Papers* 28: 57d; also *cf. Common Sense and Nuclear Warfare*, pp.38, 47, 50.

17 Between 1987 and 1991 agreements were reached on the abolition of all intermediate-range missiles (nearly 3,000) in Europe (1987) and on an equalization of NATO-Warsaw Pact conventional forces, eliminating more than 30,000 Warsaw Pact tanks (and the nearly 2:1 tank advantage over NATO) and virtually all the 500,000 Soviet forces in Europe (1991). And, remarkably, in Reykjavik (1986) the superpowers came very close to an agreement on abolition of *all* nuclear weapons. The rub was disagreement over strategic defences (Reagan's Star Wars) – US yes; USSR no. Still, we did get a treaty (START I) on strategic *reductions* (nearly 50%!) – an achievement unthinkable before Reykjavik. (See Perkins, *The ABCs of the Soviet-American Nuclear Arms Race*, Chs. 6, 11.)

18 A recent report estimates that a limited nuclear war between Pakistan and India (involving no more than 100 Hiroshima-size weapons) would kill two billion people; most of the deaths would result from starvation due to nuclear winter.

See Helfand, *Nuclear Famine,* International Physicians for the Prevention of Nuclear War.

19 See Russell's letter to the editor of *Maariv,* 26 Jan. 1963, where he characterizes nuclear deterrence as involving a 'willingness to commit genocide'.

Works Cited

Forrow, Blair, *et al.* 'Accidental Nuclear War – a Post-Cold War Assessment'. *New England Journal of Medicine,* 338 (30 Apr. 1998): 1326–32.

Helfand, Ira. *Nuclear Famine: Two Billion People at Risk.* 2nd edn. Somerville, MA: International Physicians for the Prevention of Nuclear War / Physicians for Social Responsibility, 2013.

Hoffman, David. *The Dead Hand.* New York: Anchor Books, 2010.

Kubrick, Stanley. *Dr. Strangelove or: How I Learned to Stop Worrying and Love the Bomb.* Columbia Pictures, 1964.

Perkins, Jr., Ray. *The ABCs of the Soviet-American Nuclear Arms Race.* Pacific Grove: Brooks/ Cole, 1991. 'Bertrand Russell's Preventive War Phase'. *Russell* 14 (1994): 135–53. ed. *Yours Faithfully, Bertrand Russell.* ed. 'On Nuclear Disarmament: a Letter to the Editor' [sent to *Maariv,* 26 Jan. 1963]. 1st known publication. *Bertrand Russell Society Quarterly* no. 121 (Feb. 2004): 11–12.

Russell, Bertrand. 'Russell–Einstein Manifesto' (1955). In *Has Man a Future?,* pp.54–9; *Collected Papers* 28: 57d. *Common Sense and Nuclear Warfare.* New York: Simon and Schuster, 1959. 'The Issue of Nuclear Testing' (debate with Edward Teller), *New York Post,* 6 March 1960, p.M10. 'Mistaken Identity at Thule'. *The Guardian,* 30 Dec. 1960, p.6; *Yours Faithfully, Bertrand Russell. Has Man a Future?* Introduction. *Accidental War: Some Dangers in the 1960's: the Mershon Report.* London: Campaign in Oxford U. for Nuclear Disarmament and Housmans, 1962. In *Russell Society News,* no. 138 (May 1983): 6. 'Bertrand Russell on the Sinful Americans' (with John Fischer). *Harper's Magazine* 226 (June 1963): 20, 22, 24, 26, 28–30. YF.

Bertrand Russell Society supports Marshall Islands

The Bertrand Russell Society held its 41st annual conference at the University of Windsor, Ontario, Canada on 13-15 June, 2014. Academics, students, and Russell admirers from five countries and eight US states attended. The conference featured presentations on various aspects of Russell's diverse interests, including his work in logic and philosophy, and his political writing and activism.

The Society voted by a large majority to support the recent lawsuit brought before the World Court by the Republic of the Marshall Islands, which charges the world's nine nuclear weapons nations with violation of the 1968 Nuclear Non-Proliferation Treaty. The treaty legally binds the nuclear member states to bargain in good faith for the reduction and eventual elimination of nuclear weapons.

According to the Society's vice president, Raymond Perkins, Jr., 'Negotiated nuclear disarmament is something Russell would certainly support, just as he and Einstein did as early as 1955 in the Russell-Einstein Manifesto'.

'... In relation to the United Kingdom, the Republic of the Marshall Islands invokes breaches of Article VI of the NPT, which provides that: "Each of the Parties to the Treaty undertakes to pursue negotiations in good faith on effective measures relating to cessation of the nuclear arms race at an early date and to nuclear disarmament, and on a treaty on general and complete disarmament under strict and effective international control." The Republic of the Marshall Islands contends that "by not actively pursuing negotiations in good faith on effective measures relating to cessation of the nuclear arms race at an early date and to nuclear disarmament, the Respondent has breached and continues to breach its legal duty to perform its obligations under the [1968 Nuclear Non-Proliferation Treaty] and customary international law in good faith". The Applicant further accuses the United Kingdom of, inter alia, opposing United Nations General Assembly resolutions calling for negotiations to begin; adopting a "negative and obstructive" conduct with regard to the cessation of the nuclear arms at an early date; and repeatedly declaring its intention to rely on their nuclear arsenal for decades to come ...'

International Court of Justice, 25 April 2014, excerpt
http://www.icj-cij.org/docket/files/159/18302.pdf
www.bertrandrussell.org

Reviews

Silvertown

John Tully, *Silvertown: The lost story of a strike that shook London and helped launch the modern labour movement*, Lawrence & Wishart, 2014, 288 pages, paperback ISBN 9781907103995, £17.99

When I saw *Silvertown,* the title of this book, and discovered that it was about industrial action in 1889, I immediately thought 'great, I need to know more about the London Dock strike'. How wrong was I!

I live in the region where this major industrial battle was staged. I knew nothing of it, though I have travelled many times to Woolwich Arsenal and then linked onto the London Docklands Light Railway through the very area where this all took place. This story is about industrial unrest and then action against a commercial company that today would be described as a multinational.

Silvertown is named after the Silver family who eventually established a rubber factory in this area of East London. This company started out in 1852 as a waterproof clothing manufacturer and graduated to combining rubber and the much more workable and water-resistant gutta-percha, which enabled them to become world leaders in submarine telegraph cables. Silver's as a brand eventually disappeared, which is probably why, despite the vastness of their enterprise, nothing of them except the name can be identified in Silvertown. There is no building left standing that relates to this dispute or to the people who undertook it, unlike the huge Tate and Lyle factory, which remains but was, apparently, much smaller. Silver's became the British Tyre and Rubber Company, subsequently known as BTR Industries. In 1999, BTR merged with Siebe and became BTR Siebe PLC and was eventually renamed Invensys PLC. It remains a multinational.

Whilst the company has retained its world trading capability and undergone many name changes and acquired many additional industrial processes, the workers who decided to take them on in an industrial dispute have been largely forgotten. They were unable to grow, change, and live healthy lives, having been part of the industrial success. They were asking for a very moderate pay increase. As this dispute is virtually unknown and only referenced by this work, it is more than a little obvious that it was lost. That appears so glib, but when you get into the meat of this dispute you realise that the 'unskilled' workers of Silver's asked for portions of a penny per hour in a pay rise; not the 100 pennies per pound as today, but 12 pence to a shilling and 20 shillings to a pound. They also asked for a covered or dry area to eat their food during their break. Such demands for improvement were usually met with lies, misrepresentation and obfuscation from Silver's management.

This dispute was conducted against the backdrop of the very successful matchgirls' strike at Bryant & May in 1888, and the equally local London Docks dispute of 1889. Managements across London were increasingly concerned about the rising awareness of their 'unskilled' employees and this multinational company was determined not to become part of the trend. They were proactive in establishing companies to undermine the strike by providing non-unionised workers or 'scabs'. They manipulated the press with stories alleging hourly rates well in excess of real pay. Many people believed, and I was one, that the Thatcher government politicised the police. On reading this excellent exposé, it is clear that if anyone began that process, it was the managing director of Silver's, Matthew Gray. Indeed, Tully recounts:

> 'Gray proved to be a shrewd, intelligent businessman who was not afraid to take calculated risks to advance the company's interests. And his gambles were successful. He was also to prove a ruthless class warrior when the company's interests and those of the employing class as a whole demanded it.'

And whilst Gray was fighting for his class, so, too, were the members of a 'craft union', the Amalgamated Society of Engineers (ASE). They should, of course, have been fighting for their own class, the working class, but the leadership was ineffective and unable to identify the detrimental impacts of some of their more small-minded and counterproductive policies and rules. They failed to support their colleagues working in the same factory. They failed to grasp the bigger ideas of gaining political advantage by means of solidarity. The saddest aspect is that within the trades union movement today its membership and workers generally have still to understand this basic concept. It was this strike's failure that in part led some trades unionists to realize that direct action alone, known as 'syndicalism', would not work – there was a requirement to gain traction with the public by combining the syndicalist approach with a political one of storytelling, in order to gain the understanding and support of the wider public through the media. And, by so doing, workers apply much stronger and dynamic pressures on managements. 'So what?' you may say. Well, this understanding helped to drive the trades unions and working people to establish organisations which were, eventually, to become the Labour Party.

This is a detailed book written by an academic who not only knows his subject and how to gather his research in a coherent way, but who also writes with an empathy and clear grasp of the desperations of these supposedly ordinary people who determined to take on a multinational British-based company at the centre of the British Empire and its establishment. These workers were opposed by all the British industrialists for fear of what might happen if another group of supposedly 'unskilled' workers won their dispute. Tully lays out all of the arguments and often refers to the modern day, reflecting actual successes of trades unionists born out of this alleged defeat. I take issue with him on the minor point that the Tony Blair New Labour government began the groundwork for neo-liberalism; I believe that began with Keith Joseph, a major player in the Thatcher Government. That aside, this is a thoroughly absorbing read where, despite the plethora of facts, an important story is told cogently and sympathetically, offering true insight into the appalling lives of working people. Abuses were perpetrated on them by senior managers who had the means to avoid such a dispute, the substantial company wealth to absorb such moderate requests without a problem, but their obsession with the company and making money left them indifferent and humourless, proud to be greedy, money-grabbing bastards at anyone's expense.

Many of the new practices the Silver's management brought to this dispute you will see being used today to oppose trades union industrial disputes. It is a shame, as I think Tully clearly demonstrates that the trades union movement is yet fully to realise the need for internationalism and solidarity across industrial disputes. Until that lesson is finally learnt, it is entirely possible there will continue to be variations on a theme established in *Silvertown*. This book, if read by trades unionists, could help in making that transition. It is an excellent read.

Dave Putson

'Total Historian'

Asa Briggs, *Special Relationships: People and Places*, Frontline Books, 2012, 256 pages, hardback ISBN 9781848326675, £19.99; *Secret Days: Code-breaking at Bletchley Park*, Frontline Books, 2011, 256 pages, hardback ISBN 9781848326156, £19.99; *Loose Ends and Extras*, Frontline Books, 2014, 196 pages, hardback ISBN 9781848327733, £19.99

Asa and I are roughly coevals – he was born three years after me, and both of us come from a Northern English background. But Asa's friendships far exceed mine, both in number and eminence. Of the truly great, I knew through my father Harold Macmillan, Kingsley Martin and Douglas Cole. Beyond that, I had myself close friendships with some of Asa's friends; Thomas Hodgkin, Charles Carter, Raymond Williams, Kurt Vonnegut, Dudley Seers. But most of Asa's friends and associates in political, economic and educational institutions were operating at levels far above my experience, and apart from friendship with Paul Hogarth and Diana and Tom Poulton, and brief wartime connections with Benjamin Britten and Peter Peers, nothing to compare with Asa's artistic and musical associations.

Frankly, I found the first chapters of *Special Relationships* on family names and dates and places quite boring. It was only when in 'Institutions and Individuals' he came to the founding of the University of Sussex that I got really excited. Asa avoided the pattern of appointing the top staff and leaving it to them, and instead insisted on driving the development himself with schools, rather than departments, and with the sciences and technology linked to social studies, and not just by their history, Asa's own speciality. One innovation in which I was particularly interested through my connection with Robin Murray was Asa's creation at Sussex of an Institute of Development Studies (IDS), where Robin worked and I gave some lectures on imperialism for Dudley Sears, the director. I especially enjoyed staying on the campus and running on the hills above it. He introduced a common core course for all students, a practice I followed in founding the Northern College in Yorkshire for residential adult students. And Asa encouraged mature students to come to Brighton. He supported his drive at Brighton by establishing a planning committee, capable of challenging the University Grants Committee, which had thereafter to collect the necessary statistics for the development of the new universities, which followed the Robbins Report. But after Asa's establishment of Sussex University, his chief claim to fame must lie not so much in the universities and colleges, over which he presided, as in his role from its very beginning in the founding and creation of the Open University, working on its planning committee. Many other college heads and university experts at first derided this but, after Asa became Vice-chancellor, they had to accept it.

Much of Asa's strength lay in his combination of local history and academic range of knowledge and understanding. One can give many examples, in his comparison of Manchester and Birmingham cities, of the Rowntrees and the Cadburys, of John Lewis and other retailers, of literature and technology in the *Age of Improvement*, the title of one of his most widely read books, which established him as what he liked to call himself, a 'Total Historian'. It was from Kurt Vonnegut, one of my literary gurus, who gave Asa the word *karass* as the name for a set of people who, without knowing each other, think the same way and have the same hopes and fears. It is a sense that we must all have had at one time or another, that we are not alone. Some people see this as the 'will of God'. I have no such belief. Asa's chairmanship of the European Institute of Education and Social Policy, a title Asa liked, was probably one of his most important centres of influence in his *karass*. The last lines of this book describe the 'tree of knowledge', explaining how one subject is connected with another. 'That,' he adds, 'was my preoccupation in my fifteen years at Sussex, when I knew that the University was an acorn that would grow. And it has.'

The second volume of this autobiography (*Secret Days: Code-breaking at Bletchley Park*) is about his time from 1943 to 1945, as a member of the team breaking the Axis military codes at Bletchley Park. The years that Asa spent as a cryptographer there obviously seemed to him to be of such importance as to deserve a whole volume. But the reason for such a volume lies in the largely unrecognised importance of its part in the defeat of Germany which Bletchley Park ensured. It was unrecognised because, until the 1980s, its very existence had been kept secret by all the several hundreds of people who were involved in one way or another, most of them having no idea what was going on there. Several histories have now appeared, but Asa adds the story of one particular building in the Park, Hut 6, and which German messages were decoded there and passed on to British and American Intelligence. I was particularly interested in the information they were able to give to Churchill to pass to Tito in Yugoslavia about German plans for offensives there. It is a fascinating and important story, not only because of the importance of the decoding, but also for all the characters Asa introduces. I knew only two – Ernest Barker, my friend Liz's father, and Hugh Trevor Roper, Lord Dacre, of whom Asa disapproves almost as much as I did. What is surprising is the number of people involved from Oxford and Cambridge University colleges, not necessarily mathematicians – ten alone from Sidney Sussex, where Asa was a scholar.

Asa introduces this volume with material about his time in the Intelligence Corps at Wentworth Woodhouse, my next door neighbour to Wentworth Castle, when I was Principal of the Northern College there. The layout of all the buildings at Bletchley Park and their many occupants were not known to me; this takes up much of the volume. It was here, in this very mixed range of intellects, that Asa probably learnt his enthusiasm for interdisciplinarity and the value of advance planning, which served him so well thereafter in all his university roles. Since the code-breaking activities were closed down, the buildings have gone through many uses, and it was not until 1991 that a Memorial Trust was formed. Even then its progress was chequered until the early years of the new century, when an official reopening took place, supported by Christopher Chataway and Stephen Fry, and presided over by the Duke of Kent. For 2012 a special celebration was planned to celebrate the centenary of the birth of Alan Turing, the leading cryptographer; and a model of his Colossus computer was constructed for the occasion. Asa's last words in this volume bear repetition: 'Meanwhile, interest in the remarkable personality of Alan Turing continues to grow everywhere.'

The third volume has a list of Asa's publications at the end. As with the other volumes, it has several pages of pictures. For 'what is the use of a book?' Asa quotes Alice, 'without pictures or conversations?' There is a particularly nice picture of Asa with his wife and children on page 85. This is a kind of tidying-up volume, which summarises Asa's development of 'cultural history' combining political, economic and social history with geography and dates. Thus, he wrote histories on such different fields as sport, health and retailing, as well as universities and the BBC, and called himself a scientist. He loves to think in threes and to read trilogies. As a member of the UGC he wished always to bridge the cultures and encourage interdisciplinary teamwork. The Science Policy Research Unit (SPRU) at Sussex was his instrument for much of this development. Asa did not exclude pictures and music from his cultural bridging, and the importance of wine in history and socialising. One of Asa's histories was of the Victoria Wine Company.

Along with this wide range of Asa's interests came a great number of his friends and associates. Some of them I knew well and could recognise Asa's importance in their lives: in science, Chris Freeman and J. D. Bernal (incorrectly called S. D. Bernal); in politics, Tony Benn and Harold Wilson; in music, Benjamin Britten and the Spooner sisters; among writers, Vera Brittain and Tolkien, and several academics, Douglas Cole, Eric Hobsbawm, Raymond Williams. One reference which I am sorry not to have found in his *Loose Ends and Extras* is the great kindness he showed me, when I founded Northern College, in agreeing for some years to chair the College Board of Academic Advisers. He chaired so many such advisory bodies.

The man who takes up all Asa's attention in the central chapter of this volume is John Reith, according to Asa 'Recalled and Reassessed', not only as the first and most influential Director General of the BBC, indeed the BBC's creator, but as a very great man who was not, Asa argues, fully recognised in his day. Asa referred in a 1966 Memorial Lecture to what Reith had accomplished as a 'communications revolution'. Reith's subsequent career, after resigning from the BBC, was less interesting. The BBC remains his memorial.

There is one story of Reith's role as BBC Director General that I would want to question. According to Asa's account, when Reith objected to the portrayal of Ariel's genitalia in Eric Gill's statue of Prospero and Ariel above the entrance to the new Broadcasting House, Asa's version is that the ex-headmaster of Winchester School, who was designing slogans on the entrance, reassured him that there was 'no offence in it'. The alternative version I heard from Arthur Calder Marshall, who was at the BBC at the time: supposedly, the head master of Eton, Dr. Alington, was consulted and declared that the 'young man was uncommonly well-hung', and Eric Gill had to chop off two inches from Ariel's penis.

It would be wrong to end this long review with such a story. In fact, Asa ends his life story with his love of birds. Especially, he recalls, watching the cranes in China. There they are a symbol of longevity. As he writes, Asa is celebrating his 90th birthday and the sixtieth anniversary of his wedding to Susan, and considering what flowers to give her. In China, he remarks, chrysanthemums carry a message of long life. Asa has not only had a long life, but also a remarkably rich and useful one, for which many people will be profoundly grateful. In these three volumes we can get some picture of what his life meant for him, his family and his many friends, and with it a comprehensive story of the times in which we live.

Michael Barratt Brown

Scalding tank

Clare Druce, *Chickens' Lib: The Story of a Campaign*, Bluemoose Books, 2013, 334 pages, hardback ISBN 9780957549722, £18

The Chickens' Lib group, active in Britain between 1971 and 2010, played a conspicuous role in revealing the dark side of battery farming. Founders Clare Druce and Violet Spalding (and their collaborators) went to considerable lengths uncovering animal suffering and governmental apathy, and today the widespread awareness of battery farms and their deplorable conditions owes much to their work. Not limiting themselves to the plight of chickens, they also busied themselves with farmed turkeys, quails and ostriches, to name but a few other causes. This book looks back over the group's history and provides a wealth of information that, though not for the fainthearted, remains of great importance.

Druce and co. rescued (legally) and rehabilitated birds from numerous battery farms. They petitioned authorities to face up to the grim realities of the systems in place, and to look into more humane approaches, with some success. A model for an 'enriched' cage has become much more commonplace, yet this is still a poor environment for the birds it contains. And while their efforts made an impact on European farming legislation, they so often faced a lack of will to enforce the laws. Unfortunately, this remains a stumbling block.

Beyond the obvious talking points of free range chickens and eggs, *Chickens' Lib* questions our deeper awareness of animal products. How often do we really think about poultry products that go unseen into household staples such as pasta and baby food, and where these have been sourced from; what kind of life the chickens have had, and indeed, what kind of death? Was the correct voltage administered to stun them before slaughter, or did they go to the feather-loosening scalding tank still conscious? Reading this book, you have to think back to the BNP's recent attempts to create strife over halal meat – their ignorance of standard non-halal slaughter practices, and how brutal these can be, seriously undermines their argument.

Chickens' Lib triumphs in its almost clinical precision relating the conditions in batteries, and of the animals kept there, but the writing is not entirely without emotion. Druce admits she tried to suppress the tendency to anthropomorphise, but there are points where it inevitably creeps in. It's understandable. The majority of people would empathise on some level with animals in distress; overly humanizing them is a heartfelt expression of this. The report about chickens living in an 'advanced culture' did seem like a bit of an overreach, but then again I know nothing about the intricacies of chicken social groups. My point is, even without the talk of hens' trusting eyes, revelations about the facilities Chickens' Lib visited – necrotising flesh on live birds, for one example – speak reams by themselves.

It does not get much cheerier, except when we hear about the group's comical side, which is weirdly incongruent with some of its hard-hitting demonstrations. As well as displaying pitiful ex-battery birds on Parliament Square, they have used chicken costumes and songs to get their views across. It was a risky tactic to embrace both approaches when – initially, at least – they were not necessarily seen as credible by the bigwigs. Did the more light-hearted displays jeopardise some of their chances to be taken seriously? No publicity is bad publicity, so they say, and at any rate, one need only take a cursory glance through *Chickens' Lib* to see their true credentials – how much first-hand research Druce conducted, not to mention the countless academic and legislative papers she trawled for the truth. Her approach to presenting this is excellent, accessible even without prior knowledge, and while some sections are quite statistic-heavy, the information is to the point. In particular, her critique of familiar, seemingly positive terms such as 'free range' and 'barn eggs' is galling to all those who have ever believed these were the compassionate things to buy. Some 'free range' birds are rarely able to access the outdoors at all, as there are too many others to compete against on the way to the door of their enclosure. Likewise, some so-called 'barns', while fitted out differently to the most barren facilities, 'may (legally) be so densely stocked that floor, platforms and perches are virtually obscured by the mass of birds ... likened to battery sheds minus the cages.'

It is astounding to read how Druce's attempts to alert officials so often fell on deaf ears, or else were met with limp promises to investigate her reports, always with the same results: confirmations that everything was fine at batteries she had visited and been disgusted by; glowing reports for facilities so vast that the legally-obliged checks on every individual animal could not possibly have been carried out. Her story exposes an approval system designed to green-light even the most shambolic operations in the pursuit of a profit.

It seems one of the biggest obstacles in toppling the battery system is its efficiency. Ethical concerns aside, there is little immediate, practical incentive for either the government or the public to support a reform of such a cost-effective system. According to Druce, however, the prices of 'free range' and battery eggs are not so different She notes that during a campaign against Co-op battery eggs, in 1979, they 'worked out that the price difference between a dozen free range eggs and the same number of battery eggs equated to the cost of a packet and a half of crisps or less than two and a half cigarettes'. A quick google suggests that the difference today is similar in many supermarkets. Her intended point is fine, if you live comfortably, but sadly many people in the UK are forced to live counting every penny. Couple that with misleading welfare labels that imply the animals have enjoyed a reasonable degree of freedom in their lives, and you can see how the 'out of sight, out of mind' attitude prevails.

Animal products are not essential to the diet, of course, but many choose to eat them for their protein content. Chicken in particular has been touted as a lean meat, but Druce uncovers a different story. Described in the book is an investigation into the protein content of commercially-produced meat, in 2004, which found that chicken tested 'contained more than twice as much fat as in 1940, a third more calories and a third *less* protein'. In terms of alternatives (i.e. for those who don't want to go vegan), she puts in a word for burgeoning projects such as the development of in-vitro meat, but those wary of the lab-cultured and GM food scene will no doubt take some persuasion before this is an option, to say nothing of what it may cost to produce in its early stages. In general, there would need to be a major rethink of our attitude towards food before we as a nation, or in fact as a species, lose the taste for meat altogether.

We should take the interplay of these issues to mean that there is no easy solution. It isn't economical for small, humanely-run farms to sell their produce at a rate competitive with battery eggs and meat. Until the better-sourced items do take a price dip, there is little hope that they will overtake their competitors on sales. For many people, it would be no small feat either to give up a part of their diet they enjoy so much. And let's not even go into the Herculean labour of reforming the battery system from the inside.

Entitlement and apathy abound, but *Chickens' Lib* at least encourages discussion on some things we are tacitly encouraged to take for granted.

Nicole Morris

Strength and subtlety

Adrian Jones & Chris Matthews, *Towns in Britain: Jones the Planner*, Five Leaves Publications, 2014, 324 pages, illustrated, paperback ISBN 9781907869822, £16.99

Towns in Britain starts in the English Midlands, and spreads across Britain. Nottingham, Leicester, Coventry get the treatment, before Adrian Jones the Planner and Chris Matthews, local historian and gifted designer, head off to Birmingham, Scotland and Wales. Bristol, Southampton, London and its environs precede a trio of revealing couplings, including Doncaster and Derby (railway towns), Huddersfield and Rochdale (Pennine towns), finishing with Lincoln and Exeter (cathedral cities).

Jones knows Nottingham well, with an insider's access as the City Council's Chief Planner for many years. Retirement from that position affords an opportunity for outspoken commentary and analysis of Nottingham's 'psychosis'; is it a town or a city? The conurbation spreads across 8 local authority areas, dissipating energy as councils vie with each other. In 1991, Mrs Thatcher conferred 'unitary' status on the City of Nottingham, which cut it off from the surrounding Shire County and its ratepayers. The consequent paucity of funding was compounded by the requirement, among others, to build an education authority from scratch. The City has never really succeeded in doing so and, following Gove and Cameron's onslaught on state education, Nottingham's schools now suffer increasing fragmentation. The turrets of Nottingham High School, a 'free school' established 500 years ago by Henry VIII, look down the green slope of The Forest to the Djanogly Academy, where students dig their way out under the surrounding green wire fence in a bid for freedom. The Djanogly Learning Trust has been failing the children of Nottingham since the 1980s, when a City Technology College was established outside local authority auspices, again under Mrs Thatcher's provisions. Nevertheless, it was appointed lead partner in the ill-starred Nottingham University Academy of Science and Technology, which is struggling to find students, and took over another city primary school earlier in 2014, even though the DfE has 'paused' the Trust's expansion. Last year, a coroner's court found that Djanogly Academy failed in its duty of care towards a student who committed suicide. His prolonged absences from school had not been properly recorded, it seems; nor had they been followed up with contact home. Should such dubious enterprises be trusted with children and their education?

Jones the Planner's take on Foster's Djanogly City Academy is that it is 'elegantly cool: a big statement for the area, if not one I approve of'. Personally speaking, I do approve the buildings, including the City Council's excellent new swimming pool and sports facilities behind the school. However, the kids are still trying to dig their way out, notwithstanding their bespoke surroundings. Could there be a more eloquent statement about the state of education in modern Britain?

This peroration is by way of making the point that *Towns in Britain* has a refreshingly positive and informed view of what local councils and local democracy can achieve in terms of creating liveable townscapes to support viable communities, about which the 'market' hasn't a clue

Adrian and Chris, as a combo, are knowledgeable, opinionated and humorous. One of many pictures (colour and black and white) encompasses in its caption two personal passions: paving and typography. Beneath a small picture of handsome brick and stone houses in Lincoln, it reads: 'Times New Roman – the strength and subtlety of the paving (Bailgate)'. I can hardly wait to take the train to Lincoln and promenade along Bailgate towards the Cathedral. For *Towns in Britain* is an excellent travelling companion. Just as Nikolaus Pevsner opened our eyes to what was good in the built landscape in his mammoth series, *Buildings of England*, so Jones the Planner and Chris Matthews assert the stories of modern townscapes. Doncaster looks much better with the benefit of their treatment, notwithstanding 'St George's juxta Tesco car park'. Definitely one of the best books of 2014, beautifully printed by Russell Press.

Tony Simpson

Financial Warfare

David Marquand, *Mammon's Kingdom***, Allen Lane, 2014, 288 pages, hardback ISBN 9781846146725, £20**
Stephen Graham, *Cities under Siege: The New Military Urbanism***, Verso, 2011, 432 pages, paperback ISBN 9781844677627, £14.99**
Juan C. Zarate, *Treasury's War***, Public Affairs, 2013, 488 pages, hardback ISBN 9781610391153, £34.50**

It must be rare for three major books of Political Economy to be published in English at roughly the same time, which all warn readers of the current danger to their lives of developments in financial warfare. They need to be reviewed together, all 1,200 pages, which is a major task for a reviewer who makes it a principle to read right through the books he reviews, and make careful notes of the contents as he goes along. But the three books need to be treated seriously together because they make distinct and different points of great importance for our survival. So, I will do my best to encompass them in this one review. It's written at the same time as the recent issue (no. 125) of *The Spokesman* bears the title 'Rough Violence' and is about the wars in Iraq, Ukraine and Palestine, all with a financial aspect of US dominance.

The first book is David Marquand's latest work, *Mammon's Kingdom*, which has the arresting sub-title, 'An Essay on Britain, Now'. Note the comma! The book is in fact a well-researched historical survey of the evolution of British society over the last century as still 'Mammon's Kingdom', in which the rule of finance predominates. In a quotation from R.H.Tawney, Marquand summarises it thus,

> 'Britain had undergone no inner conversion ... she carried into the democratic

era, not only the institutions, but the social habits and mentality of the oldest and toughest plutocracy in the world.'

Hence the sub-title, 'Britain, Now'. Marquand clearly distinguishes successive moves by various actors and writers over the years to establish a more collectivist spirit, drawing on the liberal tradition of John Stewart Mill and even the Conservative Edmund Burke, enshrined in the influence of Keynes and Beveridge, and the rise of Trade Unions and a Labour Party. The two world wars are shown by Marquand greatly reducing the inequalities between rich and poor, so that, in 1957, a Conservative Prime Minister, Harold Macmillan, could claim that ordinary people 'had never had it so good'.

The greater part of Marquand's book is, however, concerned with the re-establishment in the last thirty years, since Mrs Thatcher's 'Big Bang', of money power in Britain, reducing the public realm to allow for the growth of market finance in 'Mammon's Kingdom' with the domination of a tiny financial oligopoly. But, it was a risky enterprise. At the height of the boom, in 2008, Marquand estimates that British bank loans were the equivalent of five times the national output. Bank debts, not only at Northern Rock and Royal Bank of Scotland (RBS), but also more widely, were out of control. The bankers were let off the hook by national bail-outs. The Conservative Party, returned to power in 2010, with the Liberal Democrats in coalition, could blame Labour over-spending for the crisis, not bankers' greed. At one extreme there developed the super-rich 1 per cent; at the other end, the 'worthless poor'. A 'Working Class' had ceased to exist in the UK, as Marquand puts it, by the end of the century. Yet, there is a very hopeful message in Marquand's analysis, of the possibility of a 'decent capitalism', based on Amartya Sen's concept of public reasoning. This he gets from noting the growing strength of protest movements, especially among the young, on educational issues, and in political groups like Compass and Ecocide. But, it requires the devolution of power in the UK from London. 'We can't go on as we are,' Marquand concludes, with 'Mammon's Kingdom'.

This becomes only too clear in the next of my three books on financial warfare, *Cities under Siege*, with the sub-title, 'the New Military Urbanism'. Finance has not only taken over state power, but has spread a new militarism throughout urban civilian life. One needs only to see what is happening in Gaza today to recognise this. But the background to this, Stephen Graham suggests, is the growth of city populations in the last century, until today a half of the world's people live on about a quarter of the world's land; and this has not made for peaceful co-existence. The growth has not been mainly in the richer 'developed' countries, but, apart from the USA, in the poorer 'developing' lands, not so much in China, where there is a policy of family limitation, but in India, the Middle East and parts of Africa. What is happening today in Syria and Iraq, in Uganda and Sudan? Military activity does not consist, any longer, in battles for other lands, but in the control of citizens; hence, the title of the book, *Cities under Siege*. Much of the evidence of the forms of urban warfare and counterinsurgency, and their links to financial power, which Graham reveals, is little known and quite surprising, even frightening. This is a war by the all-powerful – mainly financial – groups against political dissent, often interpreted as terrorist subversion of the established order.

Every form of high technology is shown by Graham in use in 'counter-terrorism', in effect challenging democratic dissent. But some forms of control, such as the prison system, rely on old-fashioned controls. The United States, with 5 per cent of the world's people, is quoted as having 24 per cent of the prisoners. Imperial rule over colonial territories was effected by quite direct military measures. The new forms of underground dissent have led to the development of counter-terrorist operations by governments which find their cities 'under siege'. Graham's whole story of high tech surveillance and control of an impoverished city underclass in revolt seemed to be wholly exaggerated, despite the evidence of the attack on the World Trade Centre and the underground bombing, but, as I read Graham's warnings, the news comes in of young English Jihadis returning from Syria and requiring new British Government counter measures. The wealth gap between the rich and the poor is much greater in the developing countries, and between the cities and the rural areas in the USA, than in Europe, and it is in this gap that Graham identifies the threat of urban revolt in the big cities. Some of this is exacerbated by racial difference, but Graham insists that it is not always true.

The response to this threat from the big cities that Graham shows is already being developed by the US and Israeli military and it is just mind boggling. It is a particular fact of today's military exercises that the closest co-operation is between US and Israeli forces. Drones, that is unmanned aircraft, are designed to fire, not only from the air, but also from the ground in cities at electronically identified targets. This is warfare without any risk to your own soldiers, depending on detailed surveillance of city areas. This is robotic warfare, what Graham calls 'robowar', and foresees becoming the norm in intercity battles, as the technology follows the money. Already, Graham can cite its use in Gaza and Iraq, and sees weapons biting their targets like insects. It may seem like science fiction, but it seems real enough, though Graham warns against myths of precision in such plans. Some cities, believe it or not, are specially designed by the military for practising destructive measures; others are designed as safe havens for the families of the dominant military personnel, and children are taught the lesson with toy models, a more sophisticated version of the checkerboard games we used to play. And, as before, the dominant power is always in the North, and nothing is left for democratic decision making. Indeed, this conclusion of Graham's is the most worrying of all.

The total dependence of city dwellers on the infrastructure of water, drainage, transport, power, light and information services means that we are particularly vulnerable to their interruption. It gives striking workers great power, but the same goes for terrorists. The ability to single them out in the cities becomes essential to military strategy. But the result of such securitisation not only destroys democratic development but also results in what Graham calls 'dehumanising' societies in the South, which only provokes more violent response. We have only to see Isis in Iraq.

A peculiar invention of the rich North are inter-urban struggles with the South. One given a whole chapter by Graham is the car war of the armed Hummer vehicle. Short of driving in a tank, it is the safest method of urban travel. The Hummer's high petrol consumption puts even more pressure on dwindling oil supplies. The need for the North to control the oil states is increased, and the extraction of tar sands becomes more urgent. But, as Graham warns, these are severely limited options, leaving only completely revolutionary alternatives for the planet's survival.

In the meantime, we face a new kind of financial warfare from the USA, as Juan Zarate explains it in his large book, 488 pages, *Treasury's War*, published in the US in 2013. Zarate is a Senior Adviser at the Center for Strategic and International Studies, Washington DC, and was the first ever Assistant Secretary of the Treasury for terrorist financing and financial crimes, from which this book derives. Zarate's work at the US Treasury began as a response to the 9/11 bombing in the USA in 2001. It was thought essential for the US authorities to find the sources and supply channels for Al Qaeda's funding. That much of it came from Arab Muslim donors was clear, and this led Zarate and his Treasury team to Saudi Arabia and delicate negotiation with the Saud royal family, and the uncovering of intelligence agencies like SWIFT (Society for World-wide Financial Telecommunication). One important source of funding and communication from Pakistan and Afghanistan was known as '*hawara*', and this had to be dealt with.

Zarate rescued a team from a re-organisation of the Treasury, which could really build a response to the use of world-wide funds for terrorism. One of their first tasks was to deal with 'bad banks' operating illicit practices, in order to isolate rogue regimes. A particular task for Zarate's team became the tracing and isolation of Saddam Hussein's caches of money taken from Iraq via different 'bad banks' in Syria and elsewhere, in what Zarate calls Saddam's 'kleptocracy'.

At the same time, the team were giving support for Transparency International and the World Bank to help in the control of counterfeit dollars that North Korea was designing and using to pay for supplies. Zarate's team had to agree with the FBI and CIA to establish its monetary warfare role in relation to the Mafia, and had special difficulties questioning China's relations with North Korea and the gambling dens of Macau. The aim throughout was the exclusion of North Korea from the international banking system by US Treasury warnings to participants and freezing of assets in what was known as Section 311 of the US Patriot Act. In 2007, North Korea was let off the hook by Condoleezza Rice and President Bush.

The next Treasury target was Iran, whose illicit deals to counter UN sanctions on nuclear weapon development, according to Zarate, were proliferating with oil money. The aim here was to make business with Iran seem to be too risky in the USA itself as well as more widely in the Middle East. The Treasury team, now without Zarate, who had gone to the White House, stepped up its anti-money laundering and measures of isolation in an attempt to bring Iran's bid for independence to heel.

When Bush's term ended, Obama took over the same Treasury team dealing with terrorism as a new brand of 'coercive diplomacy' involving economic pressure on North Korea and Iran. North Korea's response was bellicose, with some support from China. Iran was more cautious, and Obama's US policy accepted this for a time, but continued Iranian nuclear preparation led the US to respond with increased financial pressures on banks, insurance and shipping companies, with UN Resolutions and European Union support. All this came to a head in 2012, with the threat to end all Iranian oil imports.

Before Leavey, the head of the anti-terrorist team, resigned, he managed one more financial freezing operation, against Libya, with terrorist support in Syria still a problem. Zarate sums up his story of the group's attack on the support being given to international terrorism by showing how the supporters had to adapt to the Treasury's measures against alleged rogue actors. One example cited by Zarate was Lebanon's Hezbollah's management of the used car market in Africa to make money. Al Qaeda in Somalia managed a massive drug trafficking business. But most troublesome for the United States, America's enemies had learnt how to use the Treasury's weapons back against the US financial system itself.

Zarate's last chapter is called 'The Coming Financial Wars'. Coming after the Wall Street financial crisis of 2008-9, it engages with the threat to the international status of the US dollar as the world's currency, threatened by growing Chinese power. Winning over non-state interests, essentially the big corporations, became essential. But US predominance was ended, with US financial methods taken over by others, especially China with its monopoly market position, but also by Russia with its oil and gas resources. The US is weakened on all fronts with manifold cyber attacks, but maintaining US financial power remains a key objective for all those with a stake in that power.

Michael Barratt Brown

Tribunal Jurors Adhaf Soueif, Paul Laverty, Roger Waters, Richard Falk